LIVE WELL
BAKE COOKIES

75 Classic Cookie Recipes for Every Occasion

DANIELLE RYE

ROCK
POINT

Brimming with creative inspiration, how-to projects, and useful information to enrich your everyday life, Quarto Knows is a favorite destination for those pursuing their interests and passions. Visit our site and dig deeper with our books into your area of interest: Quarto Creates, Quarto Cooks, Quarto Homes, Quarto Lives, Quarto Drives, Quarto Explores, Quarto Gifts, or Quarto Kids.

First published in 2021 by Rock Point, an imprint of The Quarto Group, 142 West 36th Street, 4th Floor, New York, NY 10018, USA
T (212) 779-4972 F (212) 779-6058 www.QuartoKnows.com

Rock Point titles are also available at discount for retail, wholesale, promotional and bulk purchase. For details, contact the Special Sales Manager by email at specialsales@quarto.com or by mail at The Quarto Group, Attn: Special Sales Manager, 100 Cummings Center Suite, 265D, Beverly, MA 01915, USA.

Library of Congress Cataloging-in-Publication Data

Names: Rye, Danielle, author.
Title: Live well, bake cookies : 75 classic cookie recipes for every
 occasion / Danielle Rye.
Description: New York, NY, USA : Rock Point, 2021. | Includes index. |
 Summary: "Live Well Bake Cookies shares 75 foolproof, delicious recipes
 that can make anyone an expert baker"^— Provided by publisher.
Identifiers: LCCN 2021001422 (print) | LCCN 2021001423 (ebook) | ISBN
 9781631067389 (hardcover) | ISBN 9780760369678 (ebook)
Subjects: LCSH: Cookies. | Baking. | LCGFT: Cookbooks.
Classification: LCC TX772 .R94 2021 (print) | LCC TX772 (ebook) | DDC
 641.86/54--dc23
LC record available at https://lccn.loc.gov/2021001422
LC ebook record available at https://lccn.loc.gov/2021001423

ISBN: 978-1-63106-738-9

10 9 8 7 6 5 4 3 2

Publisher: Rage Kindelsperger
Creative Director: Laura Drew
Managing Editor: Cara Donaldson
Senior Editor: Erin Canning
Cover and Interior Design: Laura Klynstra
Author Photos: Kelsie Jo Hillis of Kelsie Jo Photography

Printed in China

CONTENTS

The Classics

23

Oatmeal Cookies

43

Celebration
Cookies

139

Christmas
Cookies

163

INTRODUCTION

⬥────◆────⬥

Hi there! I'm Danielle Rye. You may know me from my little corner of the internet, Live Well Bake Often, where I teach people how to bake from scratch.

Ever since I can remember, I've had a passion for being in the kitchen and making desserts. When I was a kid, I used to stand on a chair and help my mom whip up a cake mix or roll pieces of biscuit dough in cinnamon and sugar to make monkey bread. I loved watching how the desserts transformed in the oven and getting to enjoy them afterward.

As I got older, I started using baking as a creative outlet. What originally started as a hobby blossomed into a passion to learn everything I could about baking. I spent years in my kitchen teaching myself how to bake and eventually decided to create a website so I could share my recipes with others.

While I was teaching myself how to bake from scratch, cookies became one of my favorite treats to create. I loved how easy it was to mix up a batch of cookie dough and how versatile cookies were too. So, when I decided it was time to write a cookbook, I knew that I needed to start with cookies!

In this cookbook, you will find a mix of classic cookie recipes—all things chocolate and peanut butter, oatmeal cookies, and everything in between. You can find a cookie for any time of year! There are also recipes for small batches, cookie bars, cookie cups, whoopie pies, an edible cookie dough, and even a cookie cake.

But I didn't want to share just cookie recipes with you. I've included all my cookie baking tips as well as a troubleshooting guide to ensure that every single recipe you make from this cookbook turns out perfectly.

My hope is that this cookbook will serve as your ultimate resource for cookies and that you will feel confident when it comes to making any recipe in it—even if you've never baked anything from scratch in your entire life.

INGREDIENTS

These are the most commonly used ingredients for the recipes throughout this book. Always read through the recipe to see what you need before you start baking.

ALL-PURPOSE FLOUR

Flour provides the structure for your cookies so that they hold together. I prefer to use Gold Medal bleached all-purpose flour because bleached flour creates baked goods that are softer, making it ideal for cookies. You can use unbleached flour if you prefer.

BAKING POWDER

Though similar in name to baking soda but not interchangeable, baking powder is used to leaven cookie dough. Just be sure that you use the correct amount that each recipe calls for; otherwise your cookies may not turn out quite right.

BAKING SODA

Though similar in name to baking powder but not interchangeable, baking soda is used to leaven cookie dough. Just be sure that you use the correct amount that each recipe calls for; otherwise, your cookies may not turn out quite right.

BROWN SUGAR

You will find brown sugar in most of my cookie recipes because it adds moisture to the dough and creates chewier, more flavorful cookies. I use light brown sugar in all my cookie recipes, but it would be fine to use dark brown sugar too. Just keep in mind that if you use dark brown sugar, it will slightly change the taste of your cookies. When measuring brown sugar, always make sure to pack it into your measuring cup.

BUTTER

Because the amount of salt in salted butter can vary quite a bit between different brands, I prefer to stick with unsalted butter. By using unsalted butter, you can control the amount of salt that goes into your cookies. If you only have salted butter on hand, simply reduce the salt in the recipe by ¼ teaspoon per stick (115 g) of butter. Make sure that you use actual butter and not margarine.

CHOCOLATE

If a recipe calls for semisweet or white chocolate to be melted, whether for adding to the cookie dough or dipping the cookies in, I highly recommend using bars of chocolate. My favorite brands are Baker's and Ghirardelli. You can typically find 4-ounce (113 g) bars in the baking aisle.

COCOA POWDER

For all my cookie recipes, I prefer to use natural unsweetened cocoa powder. Unlike Dutch-processed cocoa powder, it's acidic and will react with the baking soda in your cookie dough. I also recommend sifting your cocoa powder to remove any lumps.

CORNSTARCH

Also known as cornflour, this simple ingredient is added to a few recipes to help keep the cookies soft.

CREAM CHEESE

Always use blocks or bricks of full-fat cream cheese. Avoid using cream cheese spread in a tub because it has ingredients added to it to thin it out.

EGGS

All the recipes in this cookbook are made with large eggs. For best results, avoid using medium or extra-large eggs as this could affect the amount of moisture in your cookie dough. Most of these cookie recipes call for a room-temperature egg. If you forget to set your eggs out ahead of time, simply place them in a bowl of warm water for five to ten minutes, then use them as directed in the recipe.

ESPRESSO POWDER

I love to add instant espresso powder to some of my chocolate cookie recipes because it enhances the flavor of the chocolate. Feel free to leave it out if you don't have any or don't want to use it, but don't worry, it won't make your cookies taste like coffee!

GRANULATED SUGAR

This helps to sweeten your cookie dough and allows your cookies to spread as they bake in the oven. If you reduce or increase the amount of granulated sugar in your dough, it can cause the cookies to either not spread very well or spread too much as they are baking. For best results, always stick to the exact amount of granulated sugar called for in these recipes.

HEAVY WHIPPING CREAM

If you see a frosting recipe that calls for heavy whipping cream, also known as heavy cream, you may substitute whole milk. Just keep in mind that heavy cream will provide a creamier texture to the frosting. You may need to use less milk since it's much thinner than heavy cream. If a recipe calls for heavy cream to be whipped, like the Cherry Cheesecake Sugar Cookie Cups (page 133), make sure that it's cold. Heavy whipping cream should be at least 36 percent fat.

MOLASSES

I recommend using a high-quality unsulphured molasses, such as Grandma's brand.

OATS

Most of the recipes in this cookbook call for old-fashioned rolled oats, but a few recipes use quick-cooking oats. For best results, I recommend using the type of oats called for in each recipe. Quick-cooking oats are pressed much thinner than old-fashioned rolled oats and won't provide the same chewy texture that you are looking for in certain oatmeal cookies.

PEANUT BUTTER

Use a creamy no-stir peanut butter like Jif or Skippy in any recipe that calls for peanut butter. You want to avoid using a natural peanut butter where the oil separates from the peanut butter as this can cause your cookies to spread too much and turn out greasy. Although I prefer to use creamy peanut butter in my cookies, you can also use crunchy.

POWDERED SUGAR

This common ingredient also goes by the names confectioners' sugar and icing sugar. It's used to sweeten and soften cookie dough, and make icings and frostings for cookies.

PUMPKIN

There are a few cookie recipes that call for pumpkin puree, which you don't want to confuse with pumpkin pie filling. Pumpkin pie filling is already sweetened and has spices added to it, but the only ingredient in pumpkin puree is pumpkin.

PURE VANILLA EXTRACT

I recommend using pure vanilla extract for the best flavor in your cookies. While imitation vanilla is okay to use, cookies taste much better with the real stuff!

SALT

I use regular table salt in all the recipes in this book. For any recipe that calls for topping with sea salt, I like to use coarse sea salt.

SPRINKLES

If you are adding sprinkles to cookie dough, I recommend using the longer sprinkles, also known as jimmies. You can use small, round nonpareil sprinkles, but their color tends to bleed into the dough.

TOOLS AND EQUIPMENT

Below is a list of the most common tools and equipment you will need to make the recipes in this cookbook. Before getting started, I suggest reading through the recipe to make sure that you have all the necessary equipment.

ALUMINUM FOIL

When making cookie bars, I like to line the baking pan with aluminum foil and leave a little overhang. This makes it much easier to lift the bars out of the pan so that you can slice them. If you don't have any on hand, then use parchment paper instead.

BAKING PANS

You will need a 9 x 13-inch (23 x 33 cm) pan for cookie bars; a 24-count mini muffin pan for cookie cups; and a 9-inch (23 cm) springform pan or pie plate for cookie cakes.

COOKIE CUTTERS

The cutout cookie recipes in this cookbook were tested with 2½- to 3-inch (6 to 7.5 cm) cookie cutters. Feel free to use smaller or larger cookie cutters, just make sure to increase or decrease the baking time in the recipe accordingly.

COOKIE SCOOPS

I recommend having at least one 1½-tablespoon cookie scoop (#40) and one 1-tablespoon cookie scoop (#70). Cookie scoops help ensure that each ball of cookie dough is the correct size and your cookies will also bake uniformly. I really like OXO cookie scoops because they hold up well.

COOKIE OR BAKING SHEETS

It's best to use high-quality cookie sheets. I personally love Calphalon cookie sheets because they are extremely durable. I recommend having at least two or three cookie sheets on hand that are about 12 x 17 inches (30 x 43 cm). Be sure to use cookie sheets that are light in color; darker cookie sheets can cause baked goods to brown faster and could potentially burn your cookies. I have found that about twelve cookies fit a sheet for a 1½-tablespoon scoop of dough and sixteen fit for a 1-tablespoon scoop.

COOKIE STAMPS (OPTIONAL)

These work great for creating beautiful designs on the shortbread cookie recipes in this book. If you don't have any on hand, you can use a glass with a flat bottom to press down the cookie dough until it is in an even layer.

COOLING RACKS

It's best to have at least two or three cooling racks that are 12 x 17 inches (30 x 43 cm) to allow several batches of cookies to cool at once. Again, I recommend ones made by Calphalon.

CUTTING BOARD

A durable cutting board is great to have on hand for chopping nuts, chocolate, and more.

DOWEL RODS (OPTIONAL)

You may notice in some of my cutout cookie recipes that I recommend using dowels. They help ensure that your dough is rolled to the correct thickness and make it much easier to roll out the dough too. I recommend using ¼-inch-thick (6 mm) square dowels.

FOOD PROCESSOR OR BLENDER

A food processor or blender is great for grinding up certain ingredients, like cereal or graham crackers, for a few of the cookie recipes in this book.

FOOD SCALE

Baking is a science and even minor adjustments to a recipe can affect how your baked goods turn out, so I highly recommend that every baker have a food scale in their kitchen. Unlike measuring cups, a food scale will give you the most precise ingredient measurements, which is important when it comes to baking. Every recipe includes metric measurements for this purpose.

FREEZER BAGS OR FREEZER-SAFE STORAGE CONTAINERS

If you want to freeze cookie dough or cookies (see page 18), then I recommend keeping some freezer bags or freezer-safe storage containers on hand.

KNIFE

A large, sharp knife can help make chopping ingredients, like nuts and chocolate, much easier. I prefer to use a 7-inch-long (18 cm) chef's knife.

MEASURING CUPS AND SPOONS

I recommend having at least one set of measuring cups and spoons to ensure that you are using the correct measurements. However, for the most accurate measurements a food scale works best.

METAL SPATULAS

A thin metal spatula is great for carefully lifting warm cookies from a baking sheet and transferring them to a cooling rack. Angled metal spatulas work well for spreading frosting on cookie bars or whoopie pies. If you don't have an angled metal spatula, then the back of a spoon works well too!

MIXING BOWLS

I recommend having a set of heatproof bowls on hand in a small, medium, and large size.

OVEN THERMOMETER

Every oven is different, so I suggest keeping an oven thermometer in your oven to ensure that it's at the correct temperature. If your oven temperature is off as little as 25°F (3.8°C), it can affect how your cookies turn out.

PARCHMENT PAPER OR SILICONE BAKING MATS

I line my baking sheets with either parchment paper or silicone baking mats to help ensure that the cookies bake better. It also makes cleaning up a breeze!

PASTRY BRUSH

This works great for gently brushing things over your cookie dough, like the melted butter in the Cinnamon Roll Sugar Cookies (page 177).

PIPING BAGS

I like to keep some piping bags on hand to pipe frosting into cookie cups or on whoopie pies. I also use these to make icing sugar cookies even easier. If you don't have any on hand, you can use a plastic bag with a corner tip cut off instead.

PIPING TIPS (OPTIONAL)

While these aren't completely necessary, they will make your frosting look a little prettier. I recommend having at least one round piping tip, like the Wilton 1A, and one open star piping tip, like the Wilton 1M.

PLASTIC WRAP

This multipurpose tool works great for wrapping slice-and-bake cookie dough to chill, baked cookies to store and ship, and so much more!

ROLLING PIN

A sturdy rolling pin is best for rolling out cutout sugar cookie dough.

RUBBER SPATULAS

I have way more rubber spatulas in my kitchen than I care to admit, but I use all of them! These are great for scraping down the sides of your bowl when mixing to ensure all of your ingredients are well combined.

SAUCEPAN

A large saucepan is wonderful to have on hand for recipes like the Peanut Butter No-Bake Cookies (page 75).

SIFTER

For certain ingredients, like unsweetened cocoa powder, a sifter will remove any lumps that could potentially end up in your cookie dough.

SKILLET

If you want to brown butter for the Brown Butter Butterscotch Oatmeal Cookies (page 119), then a large, light-colored skillet will work best. I recommend one that is light in color so that you can tell when your butter is browned. If you don't have a skillet, a saucepan will work too.

SPRITZ COOKIE GUN WITH TEMPLATES

This simple tool helps to create spritz cookies in several different shapes with minimal effort.

STAND MIXER OR HANDHELD ELECTRIC MIXER

I recommend using either a stand mixer or handheld electric mixer to mix your cookie dough. If you are using a stand mixer, you will need the paddle and whisk attachments.

STORAGE CONTAINERS

If you want to store your cookies for several days, then I highly suggest getting a few glass or plastic airtight storage containers.

WHISKS

Small and large heavy-duty whisks help to ensure that certain ingredients, especially your dry ingredients, are thoroughly combined.

ZESTER AND GRATER

A zester makes it much easier to remove the zest from citrus, like lemons, limes, and oranges. I also recommend having a grater on hand for shredding ingredients like carrots.

BAKING TIPS

These are the tips I've gathered from much trial and error in my own kitchen, and I wanted to share them with you so that you can make perfect cookies every time. And if your cookies don't turn out quite perfect, check out the Troubleshooting Guide on page 17.

Read through the recipe before getting started. This will not only make the process much smoother, but you can also make sure that you have all the ingredients and tools you need to make the recipe.

Use a food scale if possible. This step isn't 100 percent necessary, but it will ensure that you get the correct measurements in each recipe, which includes the metric weights for the ingredients.

When measuring your flour without a food scale, always use the spoon-and-level method. In other words, stir your flour around to aerate it, spoon it into your measuring cup (don't shake the measuring cup!), and level it off with the back of a knife. If you end up with too much flour in your cookie dough, your cookies may not spread very well in the oven.

Check your oven temperature with an oven thermometer. If your oven temperature is off by as little as 25°F (3.8°C), it can affect how your cookies turn out. I always recommend using an oven thermometer to make sure your oven is at the correct temperature.

Always use fresh baking soda and baking powder. To test the freshness of your baking soda, add ¼ teaspoon baking soda to 1 tablespoon (15 ml) fresh lemon juice or vinegar. If the mixture bubbles vigorously, it's still good to use. To test your baking powder, add ¼ teaspoon baking powder to 1 tablespoon (15 ml) hot water. If the mixture bubbles vigorously, it's still good to use.

Use room-temperature ingredients. This will ensure that your butter mixes easily with the sugar and the eggs mix thoroughly with the wet ingredients. If a recipe calls for additional ingredients, like sour cream or buttermilk, make sure they are at room temperature too. See also the next tip.

Make sure your butter is softened to the correct temperature. You want your butter to be at a cool room temperature; in other words, it's still cool to the touch, but your finger should leave an indent if you press into it.

Don't overmix! The butter and sugar should be mixed together on low to medium speed. When you add the dry ingredients or additional mix-ins, mix them only on low speed until just combined.

Stop the mixer and scrape down the sides of your bowl. I recommend doing this once after you mix in your eggs, and then again after the dry ingredients are mixed in. Sometimes butter or other ingredients end up stuck on the bottom or sides of the bowl, and scraping the bowl helps to ensure that all the ingredients are thoroughly combined.

Avoid dark-colored baking sheets. Darker baking sheets can cause the bottoms of your cookies to brown too quickly. I recommend using heavy-duty baking sheets that are lighter in color.

Use parchment paper or silicone baking mats, unless directed otherwise in the recipe. Not only will it make it easier to clean up, but your cookies will bake up better too! Avoid greasing your baking sheets, as this can cause your cookies to spread more in the oven.

✳ **Use a cookie scoop.** Most of the recipes in this cookbook call for either a 1- or 1½-tablespoon cookie scoop. Using the correct size cookie scoop will ensure that you get the expected number of cookies, a consistent baking time, and cookies that are uniform in size.

✳ **Don't put too many cookies on your baking sheet.** Most cookies will spread a bit as they bake in the oven. It's best to leave 1½ to 2 inches (4 to 5 cm) between each ball of cookie dough so that the cookies don't end up stuck together.

✳ **Bake a test cookie or two first.** While this step isn't necessary, it can help you to see how your cookies will look once they are baked and give you some insight as to whether you need to adjust something. You can refer to my cookie Troubleshooting Guide (opposite) for more tips on how to fix common cookie issues.

✳ **Keep your cookie dough refrigerated.** If you are baking several batches of cookies, scoop them out, and then place the baking sheet in the refrigerator until it's time to bake. Remember, warm cookie dough can lead to cookies that spread too much in the oven.

✳ **Make sure not to place cookie dough on warm baking sheets.** The colder the cookie dough, the less likely it is to spread in the oven. See also the previous tip.

✳ **Bake your cookies on the middle rack of your oven.** This will ensure that your cookies bake evenly.

✳ **Want perfectly round cookies?** Roll each piece of cookie dough into a ball. Once the cookies come out of the oven, use a spoon to gently push the edges of the warm cookies and shape them into perfect circles.

✳ **Allow the cookies to cool slightly on the baking sheet.** When the cookies come out of the oven, they are a little soft and fragile. I always recommend letting your cookies cool for 5 to 10 minutes on the baking sheet so that they have time to firm up. Once they are firm enough to handle, you can remove the cookies from the baking sheets and let them cool completely on a wire rack.

✳ **Want to keep your cookies soft?** Store them in an airtight container with a slice of bread. The cookies will absorb the moisture from the bread, keeping them nice and soft!

TROUBLESHOOTING GUIDE

Let's be honest, there's nothing worse than taking the time to make homemade cookies and having them look nothing like the pictures. Even something as simple as your oven temperature can affect the way your cookies turn out. In this section, I'm sharing some common problems that can occur with cookies as well as how to fix them.

Cookies are spreading too much in the oven. Cookies can spread too much in the oven for a couple of reasons. First, the butter in the cookie dough may be too warm. If this happens, cover the rest of your cookie dough and let it chill in the refrigerator for 1 to 2 hours. You can also speed up the process by placing balls of cookie dough in the freezer for 20 to 30 minutes. Another reason could be that there's not quite enough flour in your cookie dough. You can try mixing an additional tablespoon or two of flour into your cookie dough. Just make sure that the dough is not cold, so it is soft enough to mix the flour into it.

Cookies aren't spreading in the oven. The opposite of the previous situation could be that your cookies aren't spreading in the oven and look more like balls of cookie dough than cookies. If this happens, it may be because there's too much flour in the dough. Since you can't remove flour at this point, I recommend slightly flattening the rest of the balls of cookie dough before baking them.

Cookie dough is too sticky to work with. Sometimes cookie dough can be sticky and hard to work with if it's too warm. If you are having trouble scooping or working with cookie dough, cover it tightly, chill it for an extra 30 to 45 minutes, and then try again.

Cookies are too pale or too dark. Cookies that are too pale or too dark could be the result of your oven temperature. I always recommend using an oven thermometer to make sure that your oven is at the correct temperature. If the cookies are too pale, your oven temperature may be too low, and if they are too dark, it may be too high. You can easily remedy this situation by increasing or decreasing your oven temperature by 25°F (3.8°C).

Cookies are too tough or hard. Cookies can turn out tough or hard for a couple of reasons. First, you may have overmixed when you added your dry ingredients to your wet ingredients, which overdevelops the gluten, resulting in a tougher cookie. When adding your dry ingredients, mix them on low speed until they are just combined with the wet ingredients. Another reason could be that the cookies were overbaked. I always err on the side of slightly underbaking my cookies and letting them finish setting up as they cool on the baking sheets. If your cookies are hard, try my tip of storing them with a slice of bread (opposite) and that will help soften them too!

Slice-and-bake cookies aren't turning out round. To prevent one side of your slice-and-bake cookies from flattening in the refrigerator, cut open the long side of a cardboard paper towel tube, place your wrapped log of cookie dough in it, and refrigerate it. If needed, you can even use the paper towel tube to help shape your dough into a round log.

STORAGE, MAKE-AHEAD TIPS, AND FREEZING INSTRUCTIONS

I'm not going to lie. Baking can be a real endeavor, especially with today's busy lifestyles. Here, I share how to store, make ahead, and freeze your cookies, so you can manage your baking time on your terms while enjoying the process.

STORAGE

Once your cookies have cooled completely, you can store them in an airtight container. Most of these cookie recipes will keep for up to 1 week at room temperature. However, some recipes need to be refrigerated or will only keep for 3 to 4 days at room temperature. I recommend reading the instructions in each cookie recipe to ensure that you know how to store them properly.

FREEZING BAKED COOKIES

If you need to store your baked cookies longer than the designated time in each recipe, I suggest freezing them. Once the cookies have cooled completely, store them in a freezer-safe storage container or freezer bag. If you are adding several layers of cookies, I recommend placing parchment paper between each layer to prevent them from sticking together. If stored properly, baked and frozen cookies will keep for 2 to 3 months. To thaw the cookies, remove them from the freezer, place them on the counter, and let them come to room temperature.

MAKE-AHEAD TIPS AND FREEZING COOKIE DOUGH

While I've tried to make each recipe in this cookbook as easy as possible and reduce the dough chilling time where necessary, sometimes it's still helpful to be able to prepare it in advance. Here you will find instructions for how to prepare each type of cookie dough ahead of time as well as how to freeze it.

DROP COOKIES

This type of cookie dough is one that you prepare, chill, then drop onto your cookie sheet and bake. Chocolate chip, peanut butter, and shortbread cookies are all examples of drop cookie dough that freezes well.

To make ahead of time: Prepare the cookie dough as directed, cover tightly, and chill in the refrigerator for up to two days. If the cookie dough is too hard to scoop, let it sit at room temperature for 20 to 30 minutes. Bake as directed.

Freezing instructions: Scoop the cookie dough onto a baking sheet lined with parchment paper and freeze the scoops of cookie dough for 2 to 3 hours (this will prevent them from sticking together). If a drop cookie is to be stamped or pressed down before baking, do this step before freezing. Once the dough is frozen, store the cookie dough in a freezer bag or freezer-safe storage container for up to 3 months. You can either thaw the cookie dough overnight in the refrigerator and bake as directed in the recipe or bake from frozen, adding 1 to 2 minutes to the bake time. If a recipe calls for you to roll the dough in sugar or another ingredient, then I recommend thawing the cookie dough overnight and rolling it right before baking. Keep in mind that frozen balls of cookie dough will bake up a little thicker, so if you want your cookies to spread more, just flatten the cookie dough slightly before freezing it.

SLICE-AND-BAKE COOKIES

This type of cookie dough is mixed, rolled, and then sliced and baked later (hence the name!). Examples of this type of cookie include the Cinnamon Roll Sugar Cookies (page 177), Pinwheels (page 179), and Cranberry Pistachio Slice-and-Bake Cookies (page 183).

To make ahead of time: Prepare the cookie dough, roll as directed in the recipe, wrap tightly with plastic wrap, and refrigerate for up to 2 days. When you are ready to bake the cookies, remove the dough from the refrigerator, remove the plastic wrap, and then slice into cookies and bake as directed.

Freezing instructions: Once the cookie dough is prepared and rolled, wrap it tightly with plastic wrap. Freeze the wrapped cookie dough in a freezer bag or freezer-safe storage container for up to 3 months. To thaw the cookie dough, place it in the refrigerator overnight, then remove the plastic wrap and slice and bake as directed.

CUTOUT SUGAR COOKIES

This type of cookie dough makes, just like the name suggests, cutout cookies!

To make ahead of time: Prepare the dough, divide it in half, and roll out each piece between two pieces of parchment paper to the stated thickness with a rolling pin. I like to lightly flour a piece of parchment paper, place the cookie dough on it, flour the top of the dough, and then top it with the second piece of parchment. Leaving the sheets of dough between the parchment paper, place them on a baking sheet, cover with plastic wrap, and refrigerate for up to 2 days. When you are ready to make the cookies, remove the dough from the refrigerator, remove the top layer of parchment paper, cut out shapes with cookie cutters, and bake as directed. Allow the cookies to cool completely, then top with icing if desired.

Freezing instructions: Divide the dough in half, flatten into 2 discs about ½ inch (13 mm) thick, wrap each one tightly with plastic wrap, and store in a freezer bag or freezer-safe storage container for up to 3 months. To thaw the cookie dough, place it in the refrigerator overnight, then let the dough sit at room temperature for 30 to 45 minutes, remove the plastic wrap, and roll out each disc between two pieces of parchment paper. Place the dough back in the refrigerator to chill for 1 hour, then peel off the top layer of parchment paper, cut out shapes with cookie cutters, and bake as

directed. Allow the cookies to cool completely, then top with icing if desired.

COOKIE BARS

Although cookie bars, like my Peanut Butter Cup Cookie Bars (page 72), are fairly easy to make as it is, they are also simple to prep in advance!

To make ahead of time: Prepare the cookie dough, press it into your pan, cover tightly, and refrigerate it for up to 2 days. When you are ready to bake the bars, remove the pan with the cookie dough from the refrigerator, let it sit at room temperature for 20 to 30 minutes while the oven is preheating, and then bake as directed.

Freezing instructions: Prepare the cookie dough, scoop it out onto a large piece of plastic wrap, wrap it tightly, and store it in a freezer bag or freezer-safe storage container for up to 3 months. To thaw the cookie dough, place it in the refrigerator overnight, then let it sit at room temperature for 1 to 2 hours. Once the dough is soft enough, unwrap it, press it into your pan, and then bake as directed.

WHOOPIE PIES

There are a few different ways to prepare whoopie pies in advance. To make things easier, I suggest baking the cookies and preparing the frosting one day, then assembling the whoopie pies the day you plan to serve them.

To make ahead of time: Store the cookies in an airtight container in the refrigerator for 1 to 2 days. If you are adding several layers of cookies, I recommend placing some parchment paper between each layer to prevent them from sticking together. Mix up the frosting, cover it tightly, and refrigerate it for 1 to 2 days. Allow the cookies and frosting to come to room temperature, mix the frosting well, and then frost your whoopie pies.

Freezing instructions: Freeze the baked cookies and frosting separately in large freezer bags or freezer-safe storage containers for up to 3 months. If you are adding several layers of cookies, I recommend placing some parchment paper between each layer to prevent them from sticking together. Thaw the cookies and frosting overnight in the refrigerator, then place them on the counter a few hours ahead of time so that they can come to room temperature. When you are ready to assemble the cookies, mix the frosting well, then frost your whoopie pies. You can also freeze assembled whoopie pies. Wrap each whoopie pie tightly with plastic wrap and store in a freezer bag or freezer-safe storage container in the freezer for up to 3 months. Thaw the cookies overnight in the refrigerator, place them on the counter to come to room temperature, and then unwrap the whoopie pies and enjoy them.

PACKING AND SHIPPING COOKIES

One of the wonderful things about baking is being able to share it with others, but if you have a loved one who doesn't live nearby, that can be difficult. Thankfully most of the cookies in this cookbook ship really well! Here are some tips if you want to send a batch to friends or family.

* **Avoid shipping cookies that are really soft or moist.** Cookies that have a lot of moisture in them or need to be refrigerated don't ship very well. Stick with shipping cookies that hold up better, like chocolate chip, oatmeal raisin, or peanut butter cookies.

* **Make sure to let your cookies cool completely before packing them.** If there is any moisture in your container or box, your cookies may not arrive very fresh.

* **Ship your cookies soon after you bake them.** This will help ensure that your cookies are as fresh as possible when they reach their destination.

* **Place the bottoms (or flat sides) of two cookies together and wrap them.** Wrapping the cookies in plastic wrap will help ensure that they stay fresh, and placing the two flat sides together will provide extra assurance that they won't break during transit.

* **Avoid wrapping different kinds of cookies together.** Wrap similar cookies together so they maintain their taste.

* **Ship your cookies in the correct size box.** If you have any extra room in your container, pack it tightly with some parchment paper or bubble wrap so your cookies can't shift.

* **Write "Fragile" on the box.** This step isn't necessary, but it certainly doesn't hurt either!

The
CLASSICS

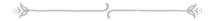

Growing up, I loved to help my mom make chocolate chip cookies. I remember how exciting it was to scrape the cookie dough off the beaters while I waited to grab a warm, gooey cookie as soon as they came out of the oven.

Even though I'm older now, not much has changed for me when it comes to cookies. In this chapter you will find some of my favorite cookie recipes that I've made countless times over the years.

From chocolate chip cookies to oatmeal raisin cookies and even snickerdoodles, I guarantee you will find something in this chapter that brings back childhood memories!

CHOCOLATE CHIP COOKIES

YIELD: 38 to 40 cookies

TOTAL TIME: 2 hours 37 minutes
(includes 2 hours of chilling time)

When it comes to the classics, nothing beats a chocolate chip cookie. The edges of these cookies turn out a little crisp, and the centers are incredibly soft and chewy. Be warned: you won't be able to eat just one!

2¾ cups (345 g) all-purpose flour, spooned and leveled

1 teaspoon baking soda

1 teaspoon salt

1 cup (2 sticks, or 230 g) unsalted butter, softened

1 cup (200 g) packed light brown sugar

½ cup (100 g) granulated sugar

2 large eggs, at room temperature

2 teaspoons pure vanilla extract

1 bag (12 ounces, or 340 g) semisweet chocolate chips

PRO BAKING TIPS

※ You can easily swap out the semisweet chocolate chips for white chocolate, dark chocolate, or milk chocolate chips.

※ If you want to speed up the dough chilling process, scoop the cookie dough onto a baking sheet lined with parchment paper, cover tightly, chill for 30 minutes, then bake the cookies as directed.

1. In a large mixing bowl, whisk together the flour, baking soda, and salt until well combined. Set aside.

2. In the bowl of a stand mixer fitted with the paddle attachment or in a large mixing bowl using a handheld mixer, beat the butter, brown sugar, and granulated sugar together for 1 to 2 minutes, or until well combined.

3. Mix in the eggs, one at a time, then mix in the vanilla extract, making sure to stop and scrape down the sides of the bowl as needed.

4. Mix in the dry ingredients until just combined, then mix in the chocolate chips on low speed until fully incorporated.

5. Cover tightly and refrigerate for at least 2 hours.

6. Preheat the oven to 350°F (180°C). Line large baking sheets with parchment paper or silicone baking mats and set aside.

7. Using a 1½-tablespoon cookie scoop, scoop the cookie dough onto the prepared baking sheets, making sure to leave 1½ to 2 inches (4 to 5 cm) between each one.

8. Bake for 9 to 12 minutes, or until the tops of the cookies are set and the edges are lightly browned. Remove from the oven, and allow the cookies to cool on the baking sheets for 5 to 10 minutes, then carefully transfer the cookies to a wire rack to cool completely.

9. Store the cookies in an airtight container at room temperature for up to 1 week.

OATMEAL RAISIN COOKIES

YIELD: 24 cookies

TOTAL TIME: 1 hour 8 minutes
(includes 30 minutes of chilling time)

Some people have strong feelings about raisins in their cookies, and to be honest, I've never been a huge fan of raisins either. But that all changes when I take a bite of these oatmeal raisin cookies. They're soft, chewy, and can easily convince someone who thinks they don't like raisins to love them! But if you're still not persuaded about the raisins, leave them out for plain oatmeal cookies.

1 cup (125 g) all-purpose flour, spooned and leveled

½ teaspoon ground cinnamon

½ teaspoon baking soda

¼ teaspoon salt

1½ cups (150 g) old-fashioned rolled oats

½ cup (1 stick, or 115 g) unsalted butter, softened

½ cup (100 g) packed light brown sugar

¼ cup (50 g) granulated sugar

1 large egg, at room temperature

1 teaspoon pure vanilla extract

1 cup (150 g) raisins

PRO BAKING TIP

You can swap out the raisins with other dried fruit, such as cherries or cranberries.

1. In a large mixing bowl, whisk together the flour, ground cinnamon, baking soda, and salt until well combined. Stir in the old-fashioned rolled oats and set aside.

2. In the bowl of a stand mixer fitted with the paddle attachment or in a large mixing bowl using a handheld mixer, beat the butter, brown sugar, and granulated sugar together for 1 to 2 minutes, or until well combined.

3. Mix in the egg and vanilla extract until fully combined, making sure to stop and scrape down the sides of the bowl as needed.

4. Mix in the dry ingredients until just combined, then mix in the raisins on low speed until fully incorporated.

5. Cover tightly and refrigerate for at least 30 minutes.

6. Meanwhile, preheat the oven to 350°F (180°C). Line two large baking sheets with parchment paper or silicone baking mats and set aside.

7. Using a 1½-tablespoon cookie scoop, scoop the cookie dough onto the prepared baking sheets, making sure to leave 1½ to 2 inches (4 to 5 cm) between each one. Gently press each ball of cookie dough down to slightly flatten it.

8. Bake for 10 to 13 minutes, or until the tops of the cookies are set and the edges are lightly browned. Remove from the oven, and allow the cookies to cool on the baking sheets for 5 to 10 minutes, then carefully transfer the cookies to a wire rack to cool completely.

9. Store the cookies in an airtight container at room temperature for up to 1 week.

PEANUT BUTTER COOKIES

YIELD: 26 cookies

TOTAL TIME: 42 minutes

NO CHILLING REQUIRED!

Is there anything better than a warm peanut butter cookie? This simple recipe is packed with creamy peanut butter for maximum flavor. The cookies always turn out ridiculously soft too.

1½ cups (190 g) all-purpose flour, spooned and leveled

½ teaspoon baking soda

¼ teaspoon salt

½ cup (1 stick, or 115 g) unsalted butter, softened

¾ cup (150 g) packed light brown sugar

¼ cup (50 g) granulated sugar, plus 3 tablespoons (40 g) for coating (optional), divided

¾ cup (190 g) creamy peanut butter

1 large egg, at room temperature

1 teaspoon pure vanilla extract

PRO BAKING TIP

The crisscross pattern created by the fork is more than decorative. It helps these cookies spread in the oven.

1. Preheat the oven to 350°F (180°C). Line two large baking sheets with parchment paper or silicone baking mats and set aside.

2. In a large mixing bowl, whisk together the flour, baking soda, and salt until well combined. Set aside.

3. In the bowl of a stand mixer fitted with the paddle attachment or in a large mixing bowl using a handheld mixer, beat the butter, brown sugar, and ¼ cup (50 g) of the granulated sugar together for 1 to 2 minutes, or until well combined.

4. Mix in the peanut butter, egg, and vanilla extract until fully combined, making sure to stop and scrape down the sides of the bowl as needed.

5. Mix in the dry ingredients until just combined.

6. Place the remaining 3 tablespoons (40 g) granulated sugar (if using) in a small bowl. Using a 1½-tablespoon cookie scoop, scoop the cookie dough, roll it into a ball, and coat it in the granulated sugar (if using). Place each ball of cookie dough onto the prepared baking sheets, making sure to leave 1½ to 2 inches (4 to 5 cm) between each one. Gently press each one down with the tines of a fork to make a small crisscross pattern.

7. Bake for 10 to 12 minutes, or until the tops of the cookies are set and the edges are lightly browned. Remove from the oven, and allow the cookies to cool on the baking sheets for 5 to 10 minutes, then carefully transfer the cookies to a wire rack to cool completely.

8. Store the cookies in an airtight container at room temperature for up to 1 week.

WHITE CHOCOLATE MACADAMIA NUT COOKIES

YIELD: 46 cookies

TOTAL TIME: 2 hours 37 minutes
(includes 2 hours of chilling time)

The base of these cookies is the same as the one used in my classic chocolate chip cookies. The only difference? It's filled with crunchy macadamia nuts and sweet white chocolate chips, making them white chocolate macadamia nut cookie perfection!

2¾ cups (345 g) all-purpose flour, spooned and leveled

1 teaspoon baking soda

1 teaspoon salt

1 cup (2 sticks, or 230 g) unsalted butter, softened

1 cup (200 g) packed light brown sugar

½ cup (100 g) granulated sugar

2 large eggs, at room temperature

2 teaspoons pure vanilla extract

1 cup (190 g) white chocolate chips

1½ cups (200 g) chopped macadamia nuts

PRO BAKING TIP
I love to press a few extra white chocolate chips into the tops of each cookie after they come out of the oven. This is optional but makes the cookies look prettier!

1. In a large mixing bowl, whisk together the flour, baking soda, and salt until well combined. Set aside.

2. In the bowl of a stand mixer fitted with the paddle attachment or in a large mixing bowl using a handheld mixer, beat the butter, brown sugar, and granulated sugar together for 1 to 2 minutes, or until well combined.

3. Mix in the eggs, one at a time, then mix in the vanilla extract, making sure to stop and scrape down the sides of the bowl as needed.

4. Mix in the dry ingredients until just combined, then mix in the white chocolate chips and chopped macadamia nuts on low speed until fully incorporated.

5. Cover tightly and refrigerate for at least 2 hours.

6. Preheat the oven to 350°F (180°C). Line large baking sheets with parchment paper or silicone baking mats and set aside.

7. Using a 1½-tablespoon cookie scoop, scoop the cookie dough onto the prepared baking sheets, making sure to leave 1½ to 2 inches (4 to 5 cm) between each one.

8. Bake for 10 to 12 minutes, or until the tops of the cookies are set and the edges are lightly browned. Remove from the oven, and allow the cookies to cool on the baking sheets for 5 to 10 minutes, then carefully transfer the cookies to a wire rack to cool completely.

9. Store the cookies in an airtight container at room temperature for up to 1 week.

SNICKERDOODLES

YIELD: 54 to 56 cookies

TOTAL TIME: 1 hour 40 minutes
(includes 1 hour of chilling time)

Most people tend to bake snickerdoodles only during the holidays, but I personally love to make them year-round. There's something so warm and comforting about the cinnamon sugar coating and the slight tanginess from the cream of tartar that makes these classic cookies irresistible.

SNICKERDOODLE COOKIES

3 cups (375 g) all-purpose flour, spooned and leveled

2 teaspoons cream of tartar

1 teaspoon baking soda

1 teaspoon ground cinnamon

½ teaspoon salt

1 cup (2 sticks, or 230 g) unsalted butter, softened

1 cup (200 g) granulated sugar

½ cup (100 g) packed light brown sugar

1 large egg, at room temperature

1 large egg yolk, at room temperature

2 teaspoons pure vanilla extract

CINNAMON SUGAR COATING

¼ cup (50 g) granulated sugar

2 teaspoons ground cinnamon

1. **To make the snickerdoodle cookies:** In a large mixing bowl, whisk together the flour, cream of tartar, baking soda, ground cinnamon, and salt until well combined. Set aside.

2. In the bowl of a stand mixer fitted with the paddle attachment or in a large mixing bowl using a handheld mixer, beat the butter, granulated sugar, and brown sugar together for 1 to 2 minutes, or until well combined.

3. Mix in the egg, egg yolk, and vanilla extract until fully combined, making sure to stop and scrape down the sides of the bowl as needed.

4. Mix in the dry ingredients until just combined.

5. Cover tightly and refrigerate for at least 1 hour.

6. Preheat the oven to 350°F (180°C). Line large baking sheets with parchment paper or silicone baking mats and set aside.

7. **To make the coating:** In a small mixing bowl, whisk together the ¼ cup (50 g) of granulated sugar and 2 teaspoons of ground cinnamon. Using a 1-tablespoon cookie scoop, scoop the cookie dough, roll it into a ball, and coat it in the cinnamon sugar mixture. Place each ball of cookie dough onto the prepared baking sheets, making sure to leave 1½ to 2 inches (4 to 5 cm) between each one.

8. Bake for 8 to 10 minutes, or until the tops of the cookies are set. Remove from the oven, and allow the cookies to cool on the baking sheets for 5 to 10 minutes, then carefully transfer the cookies to a wire rack to cool completely.

9. Store the cookies in an airtight container at room temperature for up to 1 week.

PRO BAKING TIP

If you don't have any cream of tartar on hand, you can replace the cream of tartar and baking soda in this recipe with 2 teaspoons of baking powder.

SHORTBREAD

YIELD: 32 to 34 cookies

TOTAL TIME: 43 minutes

NO CHILLING REQUIRED!

These simple cookies are much different than many of the soft and chewy cookie recipes that you will find in this cookbook, but they are still delicious! The outside is light and crisp, and when you take a bite, they melt in your mouth.

1 cup (2 sticks, or 230 g) unsalted butter, softened

½ cup (60 g) powdered sugar

1 teaspoon pure vanilla extract

2 cups (250 g) all-purpose flour, spooned and leveled

¼ teaspoon salt

3 tablespoons (40 g) granulated sugar, for coating (optional)

PRO BAKING TIP

I love to use a cookie stamp on these shortbread cookies to make them prettier. If you don't have one, you can press them down with a glass with a flat bottom until the cookie dough is in an even layer.

1. Preheat the oven to 350°F (180°C). Line large baking sheets with parchment paper or silicone baking mats and set aside.

2. In the bowl of a stand mixer fitted with the paddle attachment or in a large mixing bowl using a handheld mixer, beat the butter and powdered sugar together for 1 to 2 minutes, or until well combined. Then, mix in the vanilla extract.

3. Mix in the flour and salt until fully combined. The cookie dough will be a little crumbly at first, but it will come together as you continue mixing.

4. Place the 3 tablespoons (40 g) of granulated sugar (if using) in a small bowl. Using a 1-tablespoon cookie scoop, scoop the cookie dough, roll it into a ball, and coat it in the granulated sugar (if using). Place each ball of cookie dough onto the prepared baking sheets, making sure to leave 1½ to 2 inches (4 to 5 cm) between each one. Dip a cookie stamp in some granulated sugar or powdered sugar and press down each ball of cookie dough.

5. Bake for 11 to 13 minutes, or until the tops of the cookies are set and the edges are lightly browned. Remove from the oven, and allow the cookies to cool on the baking sheets for 5 to 10 minutes, then carefully transfer the cookies to a wire rack to cool completely.

6. Store the cookies in an airtight container at room temperature for up to 1 week.

THICK CHOCOLATE CHUNK COOKIES

YIELD: 14 cookies

TOTAL TIME: 2 hours 48 minutes
(includes 2 hours of chilling time)

There are times when you want a chocolate chip cookie, and there are times when you want a huge, thick, warm, gooey chocolate chunk cookie. When I say these cookies are huge, I mean it—each cookie uses ⅓ cup (85 g) of cookie dough!

3 cups (375 g) all-purpose flour, spooned and leveled

1 teaspoon baking soda

1 teaspoon salt

1 cup (2 sticks, or 230 g) cold unsalted butter, cubed into small pieces

1 cup (200 g) packed light brown sugar

⅓ cup (65 g) granulated sugar

2 large eggs

2 teaspoons pure vanilla extract

1 bag (11.5 ounces, or 326 g) semisweet chocolate chunks

PRO BAKING TIP

You can swap out the chocolate chunks in this recipe with an equal amount of semisweet chocolate chips.

1. Line two large baking sheets with parchment paper or silicone baking mats and set aside.

2. In a large mixing bowl, whisk together the flour, baking soda, and salt until well combined. Set aside.

3. In the bowl of a stand mixer fitted with the paddle attachment or in a large mixing bowl using a handheld mixer, beat the cubed cold butter, brown sugar, and granulated sugar together for 2 to 3 minutes, or until well combined.

4. Mix in the eggs, one at a time, then mix in the vanilla extract, making sure to stop and scrape down the sides of the bowl as needed.

5. Mix in the dry ingredients until just combined, then mix in the chocolate chunks on low speed until fully incorporated.

6. Using a ⅓-cup (3 ounces, or 85 g) measuring cup, measure out the balls of cookie dough onto the prepared baking sheets, making sure to leave 1½ to 2 inches (4 to 5 cm) between each one.

7. Cover the baking sheet tightly with plastic wrap and refrigerate for at least 2 hours.

8. Preheat the oven to 350°F (180°C).

9. Remove the baking sheets from the refrigerator and bake the cookies for 15 to 18 minutes, or until the tops are set and the edges are lightly browned. Remove from the oven, and allow the cookies to cool on the baking sheets for 15 minutes, then carefully transfer the cookies to a wire rack to cool completely.

10. Store the cookies in an airtight container at room temperature for up to 1 week.

THUMBPRINTS

YIELD: 40 to 42 cookies

TOTAL TIME: 49 minutes

NO CHILLING REQUIRED!

There's something so fun about pressing, filling, and baking these thumbprints. I love to use either strawberry or apricot jam in these cookies, but you can fill them with just about anything. Some of my other favorite fillings include salted caramel sauce or lemon curd!

1 cup (2 sticks, or 230 g) unsalted butter, softened

⅔ cup (135 g) granulated sugar, plus 3 tablespoons (40 g) for coating (optional), divided

2 large egg yolks, at room temperature

1 teaspoon pure vanilla extract

2⅓ cups (290 g) all-purpose flour, spooned and leveled

¼ teaspoon salt

½ cup (160 g) strawberry or apricot jam

PRO BAKING TIPS

✳ For a perfectly round indentation in the center of each cookie, use the tip of the handle of a large wooden spoon instead of your thumb.

✳ Once the cookies come out of the oven, feel free to add a little extra jam to the center of each one. You can use a toothpick to swirl the jam around to make sure it's nice and smooth.

1. Preheat the oven to 350°F (180°C). Line large baking sheets with parchment paper or silicone baking mats and set aside.

2. In the bowl of a stand mixer fitted with the paddle attachment or in a large mixing bowl using a handheld mixer, beat the butter and ⅔ cup (135 g) of the granulated sugar together for 1 to 2 minutes, or until well combined.

3. Mix in the egg yolks and vanilla extract until fully combined, making sure to stop and scrape down the sides of the bowl as needed.

4. Mix in the flour and salt until just combined.

5. Place the remaining 3 tablespoons (40 g) granulated sugar (if using) in a small bowl. Using a 1-tablespoon cookie scoop, scoop the cookie dough, roll it into a ball, and coat it in the granulated sugar (if using). Place each ball of cookie dough onto the prepared baking sheets, making sure to leave 1½ to 2 inches (4 to 5 cm) between each one.

6. Use your thumb to press an indentation into the center of each ball of cookie dough.

7. Add the jam to a small bowl and stir until smooth. Spoon ½ teaspoon jam into the indentation in each ball of cookie dough.

8. Bake for 12 to 14 minutes, or until the cookies are set and the bottoms are lightly browned. Remove from the oven, and allow the cookies to cool on the baking sheets for 5 to 10 minutes, then carefully transfer the cookies to a wire rack to cool completely.

9. Store the cookies in an airtight container at room temperature for up to 5 days.

SMALL-BATCH COOKIES FOUR WAYS

YIELD: 10 cookies

TOTAL TIME: 37 minutes
(includes 10 minutes of chilling time)

Several years ago, I created this scaled-down cookie recipe for my website, and it's easily become a reader favorite. This simple recipe tastes just like a classic chocolate chip cookie but doesn't make a huge batch. I've also included three other variations!

¼ cup (½ stick, or 60 g) unsalted butter, softened

¼ cup (50 g) packed light brown sugar

2 tablespoons (25 g) granulated sugar

1 large egg yolk, at room temperature

½ teaspoon pure vanilla extract

½ cup plus 1 tablespoon (70 g) all-purpose flour, spooned and leveled

¼ teaspoon baking soda

¼ teaspoon salt

MIX-INS

Chocolate Chip Cookies: ½ cup (90 g) semisweet chocolate chips

White Chocolate Macadamia Nut Cookies: ⅓ cup (65 g) white chocolate chips and ¼ cup (35 g) chopped macadamia nuts

Funfetti Cookies: ½ cup (90 g) white chocolate chips and 1 tablespoon (13 g) sprinkles

M&M's Chocolate Chip Cookies: ¼ cup (45 g) semisweet chocolate chips and ¼ cup (50 g) M&M's Minis Milk Chocolate Baking Bits

1. Preheat the oven to 350°F (180°C). Line a large baking sheet with parchment paper or a silicone baking mat and set aside.

2. In a medium mixing bowl using a handheld mixer, beat the butter, brown sugar, and granulated sugar together for 1 to 2 minutes, or until well combined.

3. Mix in the egg yolk and vanilla extract until fully combined, making sure to stop and scrape down the sides of the bowl as needed.

4. Mix in the flour, baking soda, and salt until just combined, then add your mix-ins on low speed until fully incorporated.

5. Cover tightly and transfer to the freezer to chill for 10 minutes.

6. Using a 1½-tablespoon cookie scoop, scoop the cookie dough onto the prepared baking sheet, making sure to leave 1½ to 2 inches (4 to 5 cm) between each one.

7. Bake for 10 to 12 minutes, or until the tops of the cookies are set and the edges are lightly browned. Remove from the oven, and allow the cookies to cool on the baking sheets for 5 to 10 minutes, then carefully transfer the cookies to a wire rack to cool completely.

8. Store the cookies in an airtight container at room temperature for up to 1 week.

PRO BAKING TIP

Don't skip chilling the cookie dough in the freezer for 10 minutes. This step will ensure that the cookies don't spread too much in the oven.

OATMEAL COOKIES

Some of the most popular cookie recipes on my website all have one important thing in common: they have oats in them! I totally get it too; oatmeal cookies are just hard to resist.

In this chapter, you will find the best of the best when it comes to oatmeal cookies. From classic chocolate chip to banana and even iced oatmeal cookies, the possibilities are endless.

And yes, I've even included a small-batch oatmeal cookie recipe as well!

OATMEAL CHOCOLATE CHIP COOKIES

YIELD: 24 cookies

TOTAL TIME: 1 hour 8 minutes
(includes 30 minutes of chilling time)

If you are not a fan of raisins in your cookies, then these oatmeal chocolate chip cookies are a great alternative. They're supersoft, chewy, thick, and packed with oats and chocolate chips!

1 cup (125 g) all-purpose flour, spooned and leveled

½ teaspoon ground cinnamon

½ teaspoon baking soda

¼ teaspoon salt

1½ cups (150 g) old-fashioned rolled oats

½ cup (1 stick, or 115 g) unsalted butter, softened

½ cup (100 g) packed light brown sugar

¼ cup (50 g) granulated sugar

1 large egg, at room temperature

1 teaspoon pure vanilla extract

1 cup (190 g) semisweet chocolate chips

PRO BAKING TIP

Feel free to swap out the semisweet chocolate chips for dark chocolate, milk chocolate, white chocolate, or even butterscotch chips.

1. In a large mixing bowl, whisk together the flour, ground cinnamon, baking soda, and salt until well combined. Stir in the old-fashioned rolled oats and set aside.

2. In the bowl of a stand mixer fitted with the paddle attachment or in a large mixing bowl using a handheld mixer, beat the butter, brown sugar, and granulated sugar together for 1 to 2 minutes, or until well combined.

3. Mix in the egg and vanilla extract until fully combined, making sure to stop and scrape down the sides of the bowl as needed.

4. Mix in the dry ingredients until just combined, then mix in the chocolate chips on low speed until fully incorporated.

5. Cover tightly and refrigerate for at least 30 minutes.

6. Meanwhile, preheat the oven to 350°F (180°C). Line two large baking sheets with parchment paper or silicone baking mats and set aside.

7. Using a 1½-tablespoon cookie scoop, scoop the cookie dough onto the prepared baking sheets, making sure to leave 1½ to 2 inches (4 to 5 cm) between each one. Gently press each ball of cookie dough down to slightly flatten it.

8. Bake for 10 to 13 minutes, or until the tops of the cookies are set and the edges are lightly browned. Remove from the oven, and allow the cookies to cool on the baking sheets for 5 to 10 minutes, then carefully transfer the cookies to a wire rack to cool completely.

9. Store the cookies in an airtight container at room temperature for up to 1 week.

ICED OATMEAL COOKIES

YIELD: 36 cookies

TOTAL TIME: 1 hour 48 minutes
(includes 45 minutes of chilling time)

These soft cookies are filled with warm spices and topped with a simple icing that hardens, so you can stack them. The secret to getting the perfect texture is to pulse your oats a few times in a food processor.

OATMEAL COOKIES

2¼ cups (225 g) old-fashioned rolled oats

2 cups plus 2 tablespoons (265 g) all-purpose flour, spooned and leveled

1 teaspoon baking soda

½ teaspoon salt

2 teaspoons ground cinnamon

¼ teaspoon ground nutmeg

1 cup (2 sticks, or 230 g) unsalted butter, softened

1 cup (200 g) packed light brown sugar

½ cup (100 g) granulated sugar

2 large eggs, at room temperature

2 teaspoons pure vanilla extract

VANILLA ICING

1½ cups (180 g) powdered sugar

2 tablespoons (30 ml) whole milk, plus more if needed

1 teaspoon light corn syrup

½ teaspoon pure vanilla extract

PRO BAKING TIP

To store the cookies before the icing has hardened, place them in a single layer in an airtight container until the icing feels firm.

1. **To make the oatmeal cookies:** Add the old-fashioned rolled oats to a food processor and pulse 12 to 15 times, or until you have a mix of crushed oats and some oat flour.

2. In a large mixing bowl, whisk together the crushed oats, flour, baking soda, salt, ground cinnamon, and ground nutmeg until well combined. Set aside.

3. In the bowl of a stand mixer fitted with the paddle attachment or in a large mixing bowl using a handheld mixer, beat the butter, brown sugar, and granulated sugar together for 1 to 2 minutes, or until well combined.

4. Mix in the eggs, one at a time, then mix in the vanilla extract until fully combined, making sure to stop and scrape down the sides of the bowl as needed.

5. Mix in the dry ingredients until just combined.

6. Cover tightly and refrigerate for at least 45 minutes.

7. Preheat the oven to 350°F (180°C). Line large baking sheets with parchment paper or silicone baking mats and set aside.

8. Using a 1½-tablespoon cookie scoop, scoop the cookie dough onto the prepared baking sheets, making sure to leave 1½ to 2 inches (4 to 5 cm) between each one.

9. Bake for 11 to 13 minutes, or until the tops of the cookies are set. Remove from the oven, and allow the cookies to cool on the baking sheets for 5 to 10 minutes, then carefully transfer the cookies to a wire rack to cool completely.

10. **To make the vanilla icing:** Whisk together the powdered sugar, whole milk, light corn syrup, and vanilla extract until well combined and no lumps remain. If the icing is too thick, mix in an additional ½ teaspoon of milk at a time until it reaches your desired consistency.

11. Dip the tops of each cookie in the icing, allow any excess icing to drip off, then return the cookies to the cooling rack to allow the icing to harden, which can take several hours.

12. Store the cookies in an airtight container at room temperature for up to 1 week.

DOUBLE CHOCOLATE OATMEAL COOKIES

YIELD: 26 cookies

TOTAL TIME: 35 minutes

NO CHILLING REQUIRED!

Because, let's be real, sometimes you shouldn't have to choose between oatmeal and chocolate cookies. These cookies are the best of both worlds: soft, chewy, and filled with gooey chocolate chips in every single bite!

¾ cup (95 g) all-purpose flour, spooned and leveled

¼ cup (22 g) natural unsweetened cocoa powder

½ teaspoon baking soda

¼ teaspoon salt

1½ cups (150 g) old-fashioned rolled oats

½ cup (1 stick, or 115 g) unsalted butter, softened

1 cup (200 g) packed light brown sugar

1 large egg, at room temperature

1 teaspoon pure vanilla extract

1 cup (190 g) semisweet chocolate chips

PRO BAKING TIP

You can leave out the semisweet chocolate chips or replace them with peanut butter chips or chopped walnuts.

1. Preheat the oven to 350°F (180°C). Line two large baking sheets with parchment paper or silicone baking mats and set aside.

2. In a large mixing bowl, sift the flour and cocoa powder together, then whisk in the baking soda and salt until well combined. Stir in the old-fashioned rolled oats and set aside.

3. In the bowl of a stand mixer fitted with the paddle attachment or in a large mixing bowl using a handheld mixer, beat the butter and brown sugar together for 1 to 2 minutes, or until well combined.

4. Mix in the egg and vanilla extract until fully combined, making sure to stop and scrape down the sides of the bowl as needed.

5. Mix in the dry ingredients until just combined, then mix in the chocolate chips on low speed until fully incorporated.

6. Using a 1½-tablespoon cookie scoop, scoop the cookie dough onto the prepared baking sheets, making sure to leave 1½ to 2 inches (4 to 5 cm) between each one. Gently press each ball of cookie dough down to slightly flatten it.

7. Bake for 8 to 10 minutes, or until the tops of the cookie are set. Remove from the oven, and allow the cookies to cool on the baking sheets for 5 to 10 minutes, then carefully transfer the cookies to a wire rack to cool completely.

8. Store the cookies in an airtight container at room temperature for up to 1 week.

BANANA OATMEAL COOKIES

YIELD: 40 to 42 cookies

TOTAL TIME: 42 minutes

NO CHILLING REQUIRED!

If you ever find yourself with a couple of overripe bananas at the end of the week, then this recipe is for you! These soft and delicious cookies are just like a slice of banana nut bread in cookie form.

1½ cups (190 g) all-purpose flour, spooned and leveled

1½ teaspoons ground cinnamon

¼ teaspoon ground nutmeg

1 teaspoon baking soda

½ teaspoon salt

2½ cups (250 g) old-fashioned rolled oats

¾ cup (1½ sticks, or 170 g) unsalted butter, softened

½ cup (100 g) packed light brown sugar

½ cup (100 g) granulated sugar

1 large egg, at room temperature

1 teaspoon pure vanilla extract

1 cup (240 g) mashed ripe banana

¾ cup (95 g) chopped walnuts (optional)

PRO BAKING TIP

The riper the bananas, the better for this recipe! I suggest using overripe bananas with a lot of speckles so that the banana flavor really shines through.

1. Preheat the oven to 350°F (180°C). Line large baking sheets with parchment paper or silicone baking mats and set aside.

2. In a large mixing bowl, whisk together the flour, ground cinnamon, ground nutmeg, baking soda, and salt until well combined. Stir in the old-fashioned rolled oats and set aside.

3. In the bowl of a stand mixer fitted with the paddle attachment or in a large mixing bowl using a handheld mixer, beat the butter, brown sugar, and granulated sugar together for 1 to 2 minutes, or until well combined.

4. Mix in the egg and vanilla extract until fully combined, making sure to stop and scrape down the sides of the bowl as needed. Mix in the mashed banana until well combined.

5. Mix in the dry ingredients until just combined, then mix in the chopped walnuts (if using) on low speed until fully incorporated.

6. Using a 1½-tablespoon cookie scoop, scoop the cookie dough onto the prepared baking sheets, making sure to leave 1½ to 2 inches (4 to 5 cm) between each one.

7. Bake for 9 to 12 minutes, or until the tops of the cookies are set. Remove from the oven, and allow the cookies to cool on the baking sheets for 10 minutes, then carefully transfer the cookies to a wire rack to cool completely.

8. Store the cookies in an airtight container at room temperature for up to 3 days.

OATMEAL CREAM PIES

YIELD: 20 sandwich cookies

TOTAL TIME: 56 minutes

NO CHILLING REQUIRED!

These oatmeal cookie sandwiches bring back so many memories from my childhood. One bite of these cookies and you will fall in love!

OATMEAL COOKIES

2 cups (250 g) all-purpose flour, spooned and leveled

2 teaspoons ground cinnamon

¼ teaspoon ground nutmeg

1 teaspoon baking soda

½ teaspoon salt

2½ cups (250 g) quick-cooking oats

1 cup (2 sticks, or 230 g) unsalted butter, softened

1 cup (200 g) packed light brown sugar

½ cup (100 g) granulated sugar

2 large eggs, at room temperature

1 tablespoon (15 g) unsulphured molasses

2 teaspoons pure vanilla extract

VANILLA BUTTERCREAM FROSTING

¾ cup (1½ sticks, or 170 g) unsalted butter, softened

2¼ cups (270 g) powdered sugar

3 tablespoons (45 ml) heavy whipping cream

1½ teaspoons pure vanilla extract

1. **To make the oatmeal cookies:** Preheat the oven to 350°F (180°C). Line large baking sheets with parchment paper or silicone baking mats and set aside.

2. In a large mixing bowl, whisk together the flour, ground cinnamon, ground nutmeg, baking soda, and salt until well combined. Stir in the quick-cooking oats and set aside.

3. In the bowl of a stand mixer fitted with the paddle attachment or in a large mixing bowl using a handheld mixer, beat the butter, brown sugar, and granulated sugar together for 1 to 2 minutes, or until well combined. Mix in the eggs, molasses, and vanilla extract until fully combined, making sure to stop and scrape down the sides of the bowl as needed.

4. Mix in the dry ingredients until just combined.

5. Using a 1½-tablespoon cookie scoop, scoop the cookie dough onto the prepared baking sheets, making sure to leave 1½ to 2 inches (4 to 5 cm) between each one.

6. Bake for 9 to 11 minutes, or until the tops of the cookies are set and the edges are lightly browned. Remove from the oven, and allow to cool on the baking sheets for 5 to 10 minutes, then carefully transfer to a wire rack to cool completely.

7. **To make the vanilla buttercream frosting:** In the bowl of a stand mixer fitted with the whisk attachment or in a large mixing bowl using a handheld mixer, beat the butter for 1 to 2 minutes, or until smooth. Add the powdered sugar, ½ cup (60 g) at a time, mixing in each addition until well combined, then mix in the last ¼ cup (30 g) of powdered sugar until fully combined. Add the whipping cream and vanilla extract and continue mixing until well combined.

8. Once the cookies have cooled completely, pipe the frosting on the flat side of half of the cookies, then top with the other half of the cookies.

9. Store the cookies in an airtight container in the refrigerator for up to 5 days, and bring to room temperature before serving.

> PRO BAKING TIP
>
> You can substitute 2 or 3 tablespoons (15 to 30 ml) of whole milk for the whipping cream.

CARROT CAKE OATMEAL COOKIES

YIELD: 22 cookies

TOTAL TIME: 40 minutes

NO CHILLING REQUIRED!

These delicious cookies are a cross between two of my favorite recipes that also happen to be the most popular ones on my website: oatmeal cookies and carrot cake. They taste just like a slice of perfectly spiced carrot cake, but in the form of soft and chewy cookies.

1 cup (125 g) all-purpose flour, spooned and leveled

½ teaspoon baking soda

¼ teaspoon salt

1 teaspoon ground cinnamon

¼ teaspoon ground nutmeg

⅛ teaspoon ground ginger

1½ cups (150 g) old-fashioned rolled oats

½ cup (1 stick, or 115 g) unsalted butter, softened

½ cup (100 g) packed light brown sugar

¼ cup (50 g) granulated sugar

1 large egg, at room temperature

1 teaspoon pure vanilla extract

¾ cup (75 g) lightly packed freshly grated carrots

⅓ cup (50 g) raisins

⅓ cup (45 g) chopped walnuts

1. Preheat the oven to 350°F (180°C). Line two large baking sheets with parchment paper or silicone baking mats and set aside.

2. In a large mixing bowl, whisk together the flour, baking soda, salt, ground cinnamon, ground nutmeg, and ground ginger until well combined. Stir in the old-fashioned rolled oats and set aside.

3. In the bowl of a stand mixer fitted with the paddle attachment or in a large mixing bowl using a handheld mixer, beat the butter, brown sugar, and granulated sugar together for 1 to 2 minutes, or until well combined.

4. Mix in the egg and vanilla extract until fully combined, making sure to stop and scrape down the sides of the bowl as needed.

5. Mix in the dry ingredients until just combined, then fold in the grated carrots, raisins, and chopped walnuts until fully incorporated.

6. Using a 1½-tablespoon cookie scoop, scoop the cookie dough onto the prepared baking sheets, making sure to leave 1½ to 2 inches (4 to 5 cm) between each one. Gently press each ball of cookie dough down to slightly flatten it.

7. Bake for 12 to 15 minutes, or until the tops of the cookies are set and the edges are lightly browned. Remove from the oven, and allow the cookies to cool on the baking sheets for 5 to 10 minutes, then carefully transfer the cookies to a wire rack to cool completely.

8. Store the cookies in an airtight container at room temperature for up to 3 days.

PRO BAKING TIP

These cookies won't spread very much as they bake, so be sure to gently press down on each ball of dough in step 6 to help them spread.

LEMON BLUEBERRY OATMEAL COOKIES

YIELD: 22 to 24 cookies

TOTAL TIME: 1 hour 13 minutes
   (includes 30 minutes of chilling time)

If you know me, then you know I love any kind of lemon dessert. Naturally, I had to find a way to incorporate lemon into a few recipes in this cookbook, starting with these delicious lemon blueberry oatmeal cookies!

1 cup (125 g) all-purpose flour, spooned and leveled

½ teaspoon baking soda

¼ teaspoon salt

1½ cups (150 g) old-fashioned rolled oats

½ cup (1 stick, or 115 g) unsalted butter, softened

⅔ cup (135 g) granulated sugar

1 large egg, at room temperature

1 tablespoon (15 ml) fresh lemon juice

Zest of 1 medium lemon

1 teaspoon pure vanilla extract

1 teaspoon lemon extract

¾ cup (125 g) sweetened dried blueberries

1. In a large mixing bowl, whisk together the flour, baking soda, and salt until well combined. Stir in the old-fashioned rolled oats and set aside.

2. In the bowl of a stand mixer fitted with the paddle attachment or in a large mixing bowl using a handheld mixer, beat the butter and granulated sugar together for 1 to 2 minutes, or until well combined.

3. Mix in the egg until fully combined. Then, mix in the lemon juice, lemon zest, vanilla extract, and lemon extract until fully combined, making sure to stop and scrape down the sides of the bowl as needed.

4. Mix in the dry ingredients until just combined, then mix in the dried blueberries on low speed until fully incorporated.

5. Cover tightly and refrigerate for at least 30 minutes.

6. Meanwhile, preheat the oven to 350°F (180°C). Line two large baking sheets with parchment paper or silicone baking mats and set aside.

7. Using a 1½-tablespoon cookie scoop, scoop the cookie dough onto the prepared baking sheets, making sure to leave 1½ to 2 inches (4 to 5 cm) between each one.

8. Bake for 11 to 13 minutes, or until the tops of the cookies are set. Remove from the oven, and allow the cookies to cool on the baking sheets for 5 to 10 minutes, then carefully transfer the cookies to a wire rack to cool completely.

9. Store the cookies in an airtight container at room temperature for up to 5 days.

PRO BAKING TIPS

* You can omit the dried blueberries for regular lemon oatmeal cookies.

* Want to add a lemon icing on top of these cookies? Try the lemon icing from the Iced Lemon Poppy Seed Cookies (page 109).

COWBOY COOKIES

YIELD: 50 to 52 cookies

TOTAL TIME: 1 hour 43 minutes
(includes 1 hour of chilling time)

If you love cookies filled with tons of goodies, then you are going to love this recipe! These cowboy cookies are packed with oats, chocolate chips, shredded coconut, and chopped pecans.

2 cups (250 g) all-purpose flour, spooned and leveled

1 teaspoon baking soda

1 teaspoon ground cinnamon

½ teaspoon salt

2 cups (200 g) old-fashioned rolled oats

1 cup (2 sticks, or 230 g) unsalted butter, softened

1 cup (200 g) packed light brown sugar

⅔ cup (135 g) granulated sugar

2 large eggs, at room temperature

2 teaspoons pure vanilla extract

1½ cups (280 g) semisweet chocolate chips

¾ cup (60 g) sweetened shredded coconut

1 cup (120 g) chopped pecans

PRO BAKING TIP

If you want to add even more flavor, try toasting the pecans. Just be sure to let them cool completely before adding them to the cookie dough.

1. In a large mixing bowl, whisk together the flour, baking soda, ground cinnamon, and salt until well combined. Stir in the old-fashioned rolled oats and set aside.

2. In the bowl of a stand mixer fitted with the paddle attachment or in a large mixing bowl using a handheld mixer, beat the butter, brown sugar, and granulated sugar together for 1 to 2 minutes, or until well combined.

3. Mix in the eggs, one at a time, then mix in the vanilla extract until fully combined, making sure to stop and scrape down the sides of the bowl as needed.

4. Mix in the dry ingredients until just combined, then mix in the chocolate chips, shredded coconut, and chopped pecans on low speed until fully incorporated.

5. Cover tightly and refrigerate for at least 1 hour.

6. Preheat the oven to 350°F (180°C). Line large baking sheets with parchment paper or silicone baking mats and set aside.

7. Using a 1½-tablespoon cookie scoop, scoop the cookie dough onto the prepared baking sheets, making sure to leave 1½ to 2 inches (4 to 5 cm) between each one. Gently press each ball of cookie dough down to slightly flatten it.

8. Bake for 10 to 13 minutes, or until the tops of the cookies are set and the edges are lightly browned. Remove from the oven, and allow the cookies to cool on the baking sheets for 5 to 10 minutes, then carefully transfer the cookies to a wire rack to cool completely.

9. Store the cookies in an airtight container at room temperature for up to 1 week.

PUMPKIN CHOCOLATE CHIP OATMEAL COOKIES

YIELD: 24 cookies

TOTAL TIME: 36 minutes

NO CHILLING REQUIRED!

I couldn't resist putting a fall spin on oatmeal cookies, so I decided to create a pumpkin chocolate chip version. These cookies are incredibly soft but not cakey, and they're made with real pumpkin too!

1 cup (125 g) all-purpose flour, spooned and leveled

1 teaspoon pumpkin pie spice

½ teaspoon ground cinnamon

½ teaspoon baking soda

¼ teaspoon salt

1½ cups (150 g) old-fashioned rolled oats

½ cup (1 stick, or 115 g) unsalted butter, softened

½ cup (100 g) packed light brown sugar

¼ cup (50 g) granulated sugar

⅓ cup (80 g) pumpkin puree, squeeze out the excess moisture with paper towels (see Pro Baking Tip)

1 large egg yolk, at room temperature

1 teaspoon pure vanilla extract

1 cup (190 g) semisweet chocolate chips

1. Preheat the oven to 350°F (180°C). Line two large baking sheets with parchment paper or silicone baking mats and set aside.

2. In a large mixing bowl, whisk together the flour, pumpkin pie spice, ground cinnamon, baking soda, and salt until well combined. Stir in the old-fashioned rolled oats and set aside.

3. In the bowl of a stand mixer fitted with the paddle attachment or in a large mixing bowl using a handheld mixer, beat the butter, brown sugar, and granulated sugar together for 1 to 2 minutes, or until well combined.

4. Mix in the pumpkin puree, egg yolk, and vanilla extract until fully combined, making sure to stop and scrape down the sides of the bowl as needed.

5. Mix in the dry ingredients until just combined, then mix in the chocolate chips on low speed until fully incorporated.

6. Using a 1½-tablespoon cookie scoop, scoop the cookie dough onto the prepared baking sheets, making sure to leave 1½ to 2 inches (4 to 5 cm) between each one. Gently press each ball of cookie dough down to slightly flatten it.

7. Bake for 9 to 11 minutes, or until the tops of the cookies are set. Remove from the oven, and allow the cookies to cool on the baking sheets for 5 to 10 minutes, then carefully transfer the cookies to a wire rack to cool completely.

8. Store the cookies in an airtight container at room temperature for up to 5 days.

PRO BAKING TIP

It's best to squeeze out the moisture from your pumpkin puree before mixing it in; otherwise, the cookies will turn out too cakey. To do this, line a plate with a couple of paper towels, spread the pumpkin puree into a thin layer on top of the paper towels, and then use more paper towels to blot out as much moisture as possible. If needed, you can use a spoon or knife to scrape the pumpkin off of the paper towels into your mixing bowl.

SMALL-BATCH OATMEAL COOKIES

YIELD: 7 to 9 cookies

TOTAL TIME: 42 minutes
(includes 10 minutes of chilling time)

I think you know by now how much I love small-batch cookies, so of course I had to share a recipe in this chapter too. Don't want just plain oatmeal cookies? Add some raisins or semisweet chocolate chips!

3 tablespoons (45 g) unsalted butter, softened

3 tablespoons (40 g) packed light brown sugar

1 tablespoon (13 g) granulated sugar

1 large egg yolk, at room temperature

¼ teaspoon pure vanilla extract

⅓ cup (42 g) all-purpose flour, spooned and leveled

¼ teaspoon ground cinnamon

¼ teaspoon baking soda

⅛ teaspoon salt

½ cup (50 g) old-fashioned rolled oats

⅓ cup (65 g) semisweet chocolate chips or ⅓ cup (50 g) raisins (optional)

PRO BAKING TIP

I like to place the cookie dough in the freezer for about 10 minutes, so the cookies bake up thicker. Feel free to skip this step if you prefer thinner cookies!

1. Preheat the oven to 350°F (180°C). Line a large baking sheet with parchment paper or a silicone baking mat and set aside.

2. In a medium mixing bowl using a handheld mixer, beat the butter, brown sugar, and granulated sugar together for 1 to 2 minutes, or until well combined.

3. Mix in the egg yolk and vanilla extract until fully combined, making sure to stop and scrape down the sides of the bowl as needed.

4. Mix in the flour, ground cinnamon, baking soda, and salt until just combined. Mix in the old-fashioned rolled oats until well combined, then mix in the chocolate chips or raisins (if using) until fully incorporated.

5. Cover tightly and place in the freezer for 10 minutes.

6. Using a 1½-tablespoon cookie scoop, scoop the cookie dough onto the prepared baking sheet, making sure to leave 1½ to 2 inches (4 to 5 cm) between each one. Gently press each ball of cookie dough down to slightly flatten it.

7. Bake for 9 to 12 minutes, or until the tops of the cookies are set and the edges are lightly browned. Remove from the oven, and allow the cookies to cool on the baking sheet for 5 to 10 minutes, then carefully transfer the cookies to a wire rack to cool completely.

8. Store the cookies in an airtight container at room temperature for up to 1 week.

PEANUT BUTTER COOKIES

Peanut butter cookies hold a special place in my heart because we often made them when I was growing up, so this entire chapter is dedicated to all things peanut butter.

I'm not just talking about any plain peanut butter cookies, though. In the next several pages, you will find everything your peanut butter–loving heart desires, from cookie dough to no-bake cookies and even shortbread.

If you love peanut butter, then get ready, because this chapter is bursting with it!

PEANUT BUTTER OVERLOAD OATMEAL COOKIES

YIELD: 32 cookies

TOTAL TIME: 38 minutes

NO CHILLING REQUIRED!

I figured the best way to start this chapter would be with as much peanut butter as possible. The dough not only has peanut butter but also Reese's Pieces and peanut butter chips for maximum peanut butter flavor!

1 cup (125 g) all-purpose flour, spooned and leveled

½ teaspoon baking soda

¼ teaspoon salt

1¼ cups (125 g) old-fashioned rolled oats

½ cup (1 stick, or 115 g) unsalted butter, softened

¾ cup (150 g) packed light brown sugar

¼ cup (50 g) granulated sugar

½ cup (125 g) creamy peanut butter

1 large egg, at room temperature

1 teaspoon pure vanilla extract

¾ cup (165 g) Reese's Pieces

¾ cup (140 g) peanut butter chips

PRO BAKING TIP
You can swap out the peanut butter chips for dark chocolate, semisweet chocolate, or even milk chocolate chips.

1. Preheat the oven to 350°F (180°C). Line large baking sheets with parchment paper or silicone baking mats and set aside.

2. In a large mixing bowl, whisk together the flour, baking soda, and salt until well combined. Stir in the old-fashioned rolled oats and set aside.

3. In the bowl of a stand mixer fitted with the paddle attachment or in a large mixing bowl using a handheld mixer, beat the butter, brown sugar, and granulated sugar together for 1 to 2 minutes, or until well combined.

4. Mix in the peanut butter, egg, and vanilla extract until fully combined, making sure to stop and scrape down the sides of the bowl as needed.

5. Mix in the dry ingredients until just combined, then gently fold in the Reese's Pieces and peanut butter chips into the cookie dough.

6. Using a 1½-tablespoon cookie scoop, scoop the cookie dough onto the prepared baking sheets, making sure to leave 1½ to 2 inches (4 to 5 cm) between each one.

7. Bake for 10 to 13 minutes, or until the tops of the cookies are set. Remove from the oven, and allow the cookies to cool on the baking sheets for 5 to 10 minutes, then carefully transfer the cookies to a wire rack to cool completely.

8. Store the cookies in an airtight container at room temperature for up to 1 week.

EDIBLE PEANUT BUTTER COOKIE DOUGH

YIELD: 2 cups (600 g)

TOTAL TIME: 28 minutes

NO CHILLING REQUIRED!

Do you ever get a craving for cookie dough? If so, this peanut butter cookie dough tastes just like the real deal, except it's made with heat-treated flour and no eggs, so it's completely safe to eat!

1¼ cups (160 g) all-purpose flour, spooned and leveled

½ cup (1 stick, or 115 g) unsalted butter, softened

½ cup (100 g) packed light brown sugar

¼ cup (50 g) granulated sugar

⅔ cup (165 g) creamy peanut butter

½ teaspoon pure vanilla extract

¼ teaspoon salt

1 tablespoon (15 ml) milk

1. Preheat the oven to 350°F (180°C). Line a large baking sheet with parchment paper or a silicone baking mat. Spread the flour in a single layer on the prepared baking sheet. Bake for 6 to 8 minutes, or until the flour reaches a temperature of 160°F (71°C). Remove from the oven and set aside to cool completely.

2. In the bowl of a stand mixer fitted with the paddle attachment or in a large mixing bowl using a handheld mixer, beat the butter, brown sugar, and granulated sugar together for 1 to 2 minutes, or until well combined. Mix in the peanut butter, vanilla extract, and salt until fully combined, making sure to stop and scrape down the sides of the bowl as needed.

3. Add the flour and mix until well combined, then mix in the milk until fully combined.

4. Store the cookie dough in an airtight container in the refrigerator for up to 3 days. Allow the cookie dough to come to room temperature before serving.

PRO BAKING TIPS

✳ This recipe can easily be cut in half to make a smaller batch that's perfect for two or three people.

✳ If there are a few lumps in your flour after you bake it, you can sift it, and then add it to the cookie dough.

✳ You can add just about any mix-in you want to this cookie dough! Some great options are semisweet chocolate chips, milk chocolate chips, peanut butter chips, Reese's Pieces, or miniature peanut butter cups.

PEANUT BUTTER AND JELLY THUMBPRINTS

YIELD: 40 to 42 cookies

TOTAL TIME: 51 minutes

NO CHILLING REQUIRED!

Aside from peanut butter and chocolate, one of my favorite combinations is peanut butter and jelly. This recipe is a fun twist on the classic sandwich!

1½ cups (190 g) all-purpose flour, spooned and leveled

½ teaspoon baking soda

¼ teaspoon salt

½ cup (1 stick, or 115 g) unsalted butter, softened

½ cup (100 g) packed light brown sugar

¼ cup (50 g) granulated sugar, plus 3 tablespoons (40 g) for coating (optional), divided

¾ cup (190 g) creamy peanut butter

1 large egg, at room temperature

1 teaspoon pure vanilla extract

½ cup (160 g) jam, any flavor

PRO BAKING TIP

It's best to make the indentation in the cookies as soon as they come out of the oven. I prefer to use the back of a measuring teaspoon for this step because it creates the perfect-size indentation in each cookie.

1. Preheat the oven to 350°F (180°C). Line large baking sheets with parchment paper or silicone baking mats and set aside.

2. In a large mixing bowl, whisk together the flour, baking soda, and salt. Set aside.

3. In the bowl of a stand mixer fitted with the paddle attachment or in a large mixing bowl using a handheld mixer, beat the butter, brown sugar, and ¼ cup (50 g) of the granulated sugar together for 1 to 2 minutes, or until well combined.

4. Mix in the peanut butter, egg, and vanilla extract until fully combined, making sure to stop and scrape down the sides of the bowl as needed.

5. Mix in the dry ingredients until just combined.

6. Place the remaining 3 tablespoons (40 g) granulated sugar (if using) in a small bowl. Using a 1-tablespoon cookie scoop, scoop the cookie dough, roll it into a ball, and coat it in the remaining 3 tablespoons granulated sugar (if using). Place each ball of cookie dough onto the prepared baking sheets, making sure to leave 1½ to 2 inches (4 to 5 cm) between each one.

7. Bake for 8 to 11 minutes, or until the tops of the cookies are set. Remove from the oven, and make an indention in each cookie using the back of a measuring teaspoon. Allow to cool on the baking sheets for 10 minutes, then carefully transfer the cookies to a wire rack to cool completely.

8. Add the jam to a small mixing bowl and stir until smooth. Spoon ½ teaspoon of jam into the indentation of each cookie.

9. Store the cookies in an airtight container at room temperature for up to 4 days.

PEANUT BUTTER CUP COOKIE BARS

YIELD: 24 bars

TOTAL TIME: 3 hours
(includes 2 hours of cooling time)

Although I love a good peanut butter cookie, sometimes I prefer easier desserts. These simple peanut butter cookie bars taste just like a peanut butter cookie but are baked in a 9 x 13-inch (23 x 33 cm) pan. Oh, and did I mention they are jam-packed with peanut butter cups?

2¾ cups (345 g) all-purpose flour, spooned and leveled

1 teaspoon baking powder

½ teaspoon salt

1 cup (2 sticks, or 230 g) unsalted butter, softened

1½ cups (300 g) packed light brown sugar

½ cup (100 g) granulated sugar

1 cup (250 g) creamy peanut butter

2 large eggs, at room temperature

2 teaspoons pure vanilla extract

1½ cups (215 g) miniature peanut butter cups

PRO BAKING TIP

For peanut butter chocolate chunk cookie bars, swap out the peanut butter cups for the same amount of semisweet chocolate chunks.

1. Preheat the oven to 350°F (180°C). Line a 9 x 13-inch (23 x 33 cm) baking pan with parchment paper or aluminum foil, leaving some overhang for easy removal. Set aside.

2. In a large mixing bowl, whisk together the flour, baking powder, and salt. Set aside.

3. In the bowl of a stand mixer fitted with the paddle attachment or in a large mixing bowl using a handheld mixer, beat the butter, brown sugar, and granulated sugar together for 1 to 2 minutes, or until well combined.

4. Mix in the peanut butter, eggs, and vanilla extract until fully combined, making sure to stop and scrape down the sides of the bowl as needed.

5. Mix in the dry ingredients until just combined, then gently fold the peanut butter cups into the dough.

6. Scoop the mixture into the prepared baking pan and spread it out in one even layer.

7. Bake for 30 to 35 minutes, or until the top of the bars are set and lightly browned. Remove from the oven, and allow the bars to cool completely in the pan on a wire rack, about 2 hours.

8. Once the bars are cooled, remove them from the pan and slice into pieces.

9. Store the bars in an airtight container at room temperature for up to 1 week.

PEANUT BUTTER NO-BAKE COOKIES

YIELD: 32 to 34 cookies

TOTAL TIME: 1 hour 30 minutes
    (includes 1 hour of cooling time)

Chocolate peanut butter no-bake cookies were among my favorite cookies as a kid. Anytime we were craving something sweet, my mom would whip up a batch for us to eat. This recipe is a fun spin on those classic no-bake cookies, but made with just peanut butter.

½ cup (1 stick, or 115 g) unsalted butter, cut into tablespoon-size pieces

1¾ cups (350 g) granulated sugar

½ cup (120 ml) whole milk

¾ cup (190 g) creamy peanut butter

1 teaspoon pure vanilla extract

3¼ cups (325 g) quick-cooking oats

1. Line two large baking sheets with parchment paper or silicone baking mats and set aside.

2. Place the unsalted butter, granulated sugar, and milk in a saucepan and heat over medium heat, making sure to stir often until the butter is melted and the ingredients are well combined. Bring the mixture to a rolling boil and allow to boil for 1 minute without stirring.

3. Remove from the heat, and stir in the peanut butter and vanilla extract until fully combined. Stir in the quick oats and mix until all the oats are coated with the mixture.

4. Using a 1½-tablespoon cookie scoop, drop scoops of the mixture onto the prepared baking sheets, and gently press them down to flatten them slightly. Allow to cool for 45 minutes to 1 hour, or until the cookies have firmed up. The cookies will continue to firm up the longer they cool.

5. Store the cookies in an airtight container at room temperature for up to 1 week.

PRO BAKING TIPS

✳ Before getting started, make sure to gather all your ingredients and measure everything out. This will make the process smoother and easier once you remove the mixture from the heat.

✳ I like to line my countertop with a large sheet of parchment paper. If your countertop is heat resistant you can also do this instead of lining the baking sheets.

✳ Once the mixture comes to a rolling boil in step 2—meaning that the surface of it is completely covered in bubbles—set a timer for exactly 1 minute.

PEANUT BUTTER SHORTBREAD

YIELD: 44 cookies

TOTAL TIME: 48 minutes

NO CHILLING REQUIRED!

If you love shortbread cookies, you are going to adore the fun spin on this shortbread recipe! Filled with peanut butter, these simple cookies are slightly crunchy on the outside but will melt in your mouth.

1 cup (2 sticks, or 230 g) unsalted butter, softened

½ cup (100 g) packed light brown sugar

½ cup (125 g) creamy peanut butter

1 teaspoon pure vanilla extract

2 cups (250 g) all-purpose flour, spooned and leveled

¼ cup (32 g) cornstarch

¼ teaspoon salt

¼ cup (50 g) granulated sugar

1. Preheat the oven to 350°F (180°C). Line large baking sheets with parchment paper or silicone baking mats and set aside.

2. In the bowl of a stand mixer fitted with the paddle attachment or in a large mixing bowl using a handheld mixer, beat the butter for about 1 minute, or until smooth. Mix in the brown sugar for another minute, or until fully incorporated into the butter.

3. Mix in the peanut butter and vanilla extract until fully combined, making sure to stop and scrape down the sides of the bowl as needed.

4. Sift the flour, cornstarch, and salt into the wet ingredients and mix on low-medium speed until just combined.

5. Place the granulated sugar in a small bowl. Using a 1-tablespoon cookie scoop, scoop the cookie dough, roll it into a ball, and coat it in the granulated sugar. Place each ball of cookie dough onto the prepared baking sheets, making sure to leave 1½ to 2 inches (4 to 5 cm) between each one.

6. Using a cookie stamp, press down each ball of cookie dough.

7. Bake for 11 to 13 minutes, or until the tops of the cookies are set and the edges are lightly browned. Remove from the oven, and allow the cookies to cool on the baking sheets for 5 to 10 minutes, then carefully transfer the cookies to a wire rack to cool completely.

8. Store the cookies in an airtight container at room temperature for up to 1 week.

PRO BAKING TIPS

* Want to add some chocolate to these cookies? Melt 12 ounces (340 g) of semisweet chocolate, dip half of each cookie into the chocolate, place on a baking sheet lined with parchment paper, and chill for 20 to 30 minutes, or until the chocolate is firm.

* I love to use a cookie stamp on these shortbread cookies to make them prettier. If you don't have one, you can press them down with a glass cup with a flat bottom.

PEANUT BUTTER BLOSSOMS

YIELD: 24 cookies

TOTAL TIME: 42 minutes

NO CHILLING REQUIRED!

When it comes to peanut butter cookies, you can't beat a classic peanut butter blossom! This simple recipe comes together quickly and creates the softest peanut butter cookies you will ever try.

1½ cups (190 g) all-purpose flour, spooned and leveled

½ teaspoon baking soda

¼ teaspoon salt

½ cup (1 stick, or 115 g) unsalted butter, softened

½ cup (100 g) packed light brown sugar

¼ cup (50 g) granulated sugar, plus 3 tablespoons (40 g) for coating (optional), divided

¾ cup (190 g) creamy peanut butter

1 large egg, at room temperature

1 teaspoon pure vanilla extract

24 Hershey's Kisses, unwrapped

PRO BAKING TIP

It's best to press the chocolate kisses into the cookies right after they come out of the oven. To make this step easier, I suggest unwrapping all the Hershey's Kisses ahead of time.

1. Preheat the oven to 350°F (180°C). Line two large baking sheets with parchment paper or silicone baking mats and set aside.

2. In a large mixing bowl, whisk together the flour, baking soda, and salt until well combined. Set aside.

3. In the bowl of a stand mixer fitted with the paddle attachment or in a large mixing bowl using a handheld mixer, beat the butter, brown sugar, and ¼ cup (50 g) of the granulated sugar together for 1 to 2 minutes, or until well combined.

4. Mix in the peanut butter, egg, and vanilla extract until fully combined, making sure to stop and scrape down the sides of the bowl as needed.

5. Mix in the dry ingredients until just combined.

6. Place the remaining 3 tablespoons (40 g) granulated sugar (if using) in a small bowl. Using a 1½-tablespoon cookie scoop, scoop the cookie dough, roll it into a ball, and coat it in the granulated sugar (if using). Place each ball of cookie dough onto the prepared baking sheets, making sure to leave 1½ to 2 inches (4 to 5 cm) between each one.

7. Bake for 9 to 12 minutes, or until the tops of the cookies are set. Remove from the oven, and gently press a Hershey's Kiss into the top of each cookie. Allow the cookies to cool on the baking sheets for 10 minutes, then carefully transfer the cookies to a wire rack to cool completely.

8. Store the cookies in an airtight container at room temperature for up to 1 week.

FLOURLESS PEANUT BUTTER COOKIES

YIELD: 14 cookies

TOTAL TIME: 30 minutes

NO CHILLING REQUIRED!

Whenever I'm craving a cookie but am short on time, I love to throw together these easy flourless peanut butter cookies. They are made with just four ingredients but taste like a regular peanut butter cookie. And as a bonus, they're naturally gluten-free!

1 cup (250 g) creamy peanut butter

⅔ cup (135 g) granulated sugar

1 large egg, at room temperature

1 teaspoon pure vanilla extract

1. Preheat the oven to 350°F (180°C). Line a large baking sheet with parchment paper or a silicone baking mat and set aside.

2. In a large mixing bowl using a handheld mixer, beat the peanut butter, granulated sugar, egg, and vanilla extract until fully combined.

3. Using a 1½-tablespoon cookie scoop, scoop the cookie dough onto the prepared baking sheet, making sure to leave 1½ to 2 inches (4 to 5 cm) between each one. Roll the cookie dough into balls and press each one down with the tines of a fork to make a crisscross pattern.

4. Bake for 12 to 15 minutes, or until the tops of the cookies are set. Remove from the oven, and allow the cookies to cool on the baking sheet for 15 to 20 minutes, then carefully transfer the cookies to a wire rack to cool completely.

5. Store the cookies in an airtight container at room temperature for up to 1 week.

PRO BAKING TIPS

✳ The crisscross pattern created by the fork is more than decorative. It helps these cookies spread in the oven.

✳ Since these cookies don't have any flour in them, they will be fragile when they are warm. Make sure to let them cool for at least 15 to 20 minutes before removing them from the baking sheet.

SMALL-BATCH PEANUT BUTTER COOKIES

YIELD: 7 cookies

TOTAL TIME: 31 minutes

NO CHILLING REQUIRED!

While I love a good peanut butter cookie, sometimes I don't feel like making a full batch and having them just sit around the house tempting me. This simple peanut butter cookie recipe is perfect if you are craving a cookie but don't want to overindulge.

2 tablespoons (30 g) unsalted butter, softened

3 tablespoons (40g) packed light brown sugar

1 tablespoon (13 g) granulated sugar

3 tablespoons (50 g) creamy peanut butter

1 large egg yolk, at room temperature

¼ teaspoon pure vanilla extract

¼ cup plus 2 tablespoons (50 g) all-purpose flour, spooned and leveled

¼ teaspoon baking soda

Tiny pinch of salt (optional)

PRO BAKING TIP

Don't have a handheld mixer? You can easily cream the butter and sugars together with a fork, and then mix in the other ingredients.

1. Preheat the oven to 350°F (180°C). Line a large baking sheet with parchment paper or a silicone baking mat and set aside.

2. In a medium mixing bowl using a handheld mixer, beat the butter, brown sugar, and granulated sugar together until well combined. Mix in the peanut butter, egg yolk, and vanilla extract until fully combined.

3. Mix in the flour, baking soda, and salt (if using) until just combined, making sure to stop and scrape down the sides of the bowl as needed.

4. Using a 1½-tablespoon cookie scoop, scoop the cookie dough onto the prepared baking sheet, making sure to leave 1½ to 2 inches (4 to 5 cm) between each one. Gently press down on the top of each one with the tines of a fork to make a small crisscross pattern.

5. Bake for 9 to 11 minutes, or until the tops of the cookies are set. Remove from the oven, and allow the cookies to cool on the baking sheet for 5 to 10 minutes, then carefully transfer the cookies to a wire rack to cool completely.

6. Store the cookies in an airtight container at room temperature for up to 1 week.

CHOCOLATE COOKIES

You didn't think I could skip over chocolate, did you?
Of course not!

Chocolate is one of my favorite treats, so I knew that I had to include as many chocolate recipes as I could in this cookbook. In this chapter, you will find a mix of classic chocolate cookies with fun twists, cutout sugar cookies, and even whoopie pies.

If you are a chocolate lover like myself, you will want to indulge in this next chapter.

BROWNIE COOKIES

YIELD: 30 cookies

TOTAL TIME: 1 hour 41 minutes
(includes 1 hour of chilling time)

The name of this cookie says it all. These cookies taste exactly like everyone's favorite part of a batch of brownies—the corner pieces!

1 cup (125 g) all-purpose flour, spooned and leveled

¼ cup (22 g) natural unsweetened cocoa powder

1 teaspoon baking powder

¼ teaspoon salt

6 tablespoons (85 g) unsalted butter, softened

¾ cup (150 g) packed light brown sugar

½ cup (100 g) granulated sugar

2 large eggs, at room temperature

1 teaspoon pure vanilla extract

8 ounces (226 g) semisweet chocolate, melted and slightly cooled

PRO BAKING TIP

If you want to add a little something extra to these cookies, mix 1 cup (120 g) of chopped walnuts into the cookie dough after you have mixed in the dry ingredients in step 4.

1. In a large mixing bowl, sift the flour and cocoa powder together, then whisk in the baking powder and salt until well combined. Set aside.

2. In the bowl of a stand mixer fitted with the paddle attachment or in a large mixing bowl using a handheld mixer, beat the butter, brown sugar, and granulated sugar together for 1 to 2 minutes, or until well combined.

3. Mix in the eggs and vanilla extract, making sure to stop and scrape down the sides of the bowl as needed. Add the melted chocolate and continue mixing until fully combined.

4. Mix in the dry ingredients until just combined.

5. Cover tightly and refrigerate for at least 1 hour.

6. Preheat the oven to 350°F (180°C). Line large baking sheets with parchment paper or silicone baking mats and set aside.

7. Using a 1½-tablespoon cookie scoop, scoop the cookie dough, roll it into a ball, and place it onto the prepared baking sheets, making sure to leave 1½ to 2 inches (4 to 5 cm) between each one.

8. Bake for 9 to 11 minutes, or until the tops of the cookies are set and start to crack. Remove from the oven, and allow the cookies to cool on the baking sheets for 10 minutes, then carefully transfer the cookies to a wire rack to cool completely.

9. Store the cookies in an airtight container at room temperature for up to 1 week.

DOUBLE CHOCOLATE M&M'S COOKIES

YIELD: 26 cookies

TOTAL TIME: 1 hour 6 minutes
(includes 30 minutes of chilling time)

Because you can't go wrong with a little extra chocolate, these soft chocolate cookies are filled to the brim with chocolate chips and M&M's candies.

- 1¼ cups (160 g) all-purpose flour, spooned and leveled
- ⅓ cup (30 g) natural unsweetened cocoa powder
- ½ teaspoon baking soda
- ¼ teaspoon salt
- ½ cup (1 stick, or 115 g) unsalted butter, softened
- ½ cup (100 g) packed light brown sugar
- ½ cup (100 g) granulated sugar
- 1 large egg, at room temperature
- 1 teaspoon pure vanilla extract
- ¾ cup (140 g) semisweet chocolate chips
- ½ cup (105 g) M&M's Minis Milk Chocolate Baking Bits

PRO BAKING TIP

For an extra pop of color, add a few M&M's Minis Baking Bits to the top of each ball of cookie dough before putting the baking sheet in the oven.

1. In a large mixing bowl, sift the flour and cocoa powder together, then whisk in the baking soda and salt until well combined. Set aside.

2. In the bowl of a stand mixer fitted with the paddle attachment or in a large mixing bowl using a handheld mixer, beat the butter, brown sugar, and granulated sugar together for 1 to 2 minutes, or until well combined.

3. Mix in the egg and vanilla extract until fully combined, making sure to stop and scrape down the sides of the bowl as needed.

4. Mix in the dry ingredients until just combined, then gently stir in the chocolate chips and M&M's Minis Baking Bits until fully incorporated.

5. Cover tightly and refrigerate for at least 30 minutes.

6. Meanwhile, preheat the oven to 350°F (180°C). Line large baking sheets with parchment paper or silicone baking mats and set aside.

7. Using a 1½-tablespoon cookie scoop, scoop the cookie dough onto the prepared baking sheets, making sure to leave 1½ to 2 inches (4 to 5 cm) between each one.

8. Bake for 9 to 11 minutes, or until the tops of the cookie are set. Remove from the oven, and allow the cookies to cool on the baking sheets for 5 to 10 minutes, then carefully transfer the cookies to a wire rack to cool completely.

9. Store the cookies in an airtight container at room temperature for up to 1 week.

CHOCOLATE NUTELLA COOKIES

YIELD: 28 to 30 cookies

TOTAL TIME: 38 minutes

NO CHILLING REQUIRED!

Nutella lovers rejoice! These chocolate cookies feature three different kinds of chocolate in them: chocolate hazelnut spread, a touch of cocoa powder, and chocolate chips. These cookies are a chocolate lover's dream come true!

1⅔ cups (210 g) all-purpose flour, spooned and leveled

3 tablespoons (16 g) natural unsweetened cocoa powder

1 teaspoon cornstarch

½ teaspoon baking soda

½ teaspoon baking powder

¼ teaspoon salt

½ cup (1 stick, or 115 g) unsalted butter, softened

¾ cup (150 g) packed light brown sugar

½ cup (145 g) Nutella

1 large egg, at room temperature

1 teaspoon pure vanilla extract

1 cup (190 g) semisweet chocolate chips

PRO BAKING TIP

If you prefer plain Nutella cookies, simply leave out the semisweet chocolate chips.

1. Preheat the oven to 350°F (180°C). Line large baking sheets with parchment paper or silicone baking mats and set aside.

2. In a large mixing bowl, sift the flour and cocoa powder together, then whisk in the cornstarch, baking soda, baking powder, and salt until well combined. Set aside.

3. In the bowl of a stand mixer fitted with the paddle attachment or in a large mixing bowl using a handheld mixer, beat the butter and brown sugar together for 1 to 2 minutes, or until well combined.

4. Mix in the Nutella, egg, and vanilla extract until fully combined, making sure to stop and scrape down the sides of the bowl as needed.

5. Mix in the dry ingredients until just combined, then mix in the chocolate chips on low speed until fully incorporated.

6. Using a 1½-tablespoon cookie scoop, scoop the cookie dough onto the prepared baking sheets, making sure to leave 1½ to 2 inches (4 to 5 cm) between each one.

7. Bake for 10 to 13 minutes, or until the tops of the cookies are set. Remove from the oven, and allow the cookies to cool on the baking sheets for 5 to 10 minutes, then carefully transfer the cookies to a wire rack to cool completely.

8. Store the cookies in an airtight container at room temperature for up to 1 week.

FLOURLESS CHOCOLATE COOKIES

YIELD: 24 to 26 cookies

TOTAL TIME: 39 minutes

NO CHILLING REQUIRED!

Unlike all the other cookie recipes in this chapter, these chocolate cookies are completely flourless. But don't let that fool you; these cookies are still chocolatey, light, and superchewy. And as a bonus, they're naturally gluten-free!

3 cups (360 g) powdered sugar

¾ cup (65 g) natural unsweetened cocoa powder

½ teaspoon instant espresso powder (optional)

¼ teaspoon salt

2 large egg whites, at room temperature

1 large egg, at room temperature

1½ teaspoons pure vanilla extract

PRO BAKING TIP

These cookies will be soft and fragile while they are warm. Make sure to let the cookies cool completely on the baking sheets before you remove them.

1. Preheat the oven to 350°F (180°C). Line two large baking sheets with parchment paper or silicone baking mats and set aside.

2. In a medium mixing bowl, sift the powdered sugar and unsweetened cocoa powder together, then whisk in the instant espresso powder (if using) and salt until well combined. Set aside.

3. In a separate medium mixing bowl, whisk together the egg whites, egg, and vanilla extract until fully combined.

4. Add the wet ingredients to the dry ingredients, and stir until the mixture is fully combined and smooth.

5. Using a 1-tablespoon cookie scoop, scoop the cookie dough onto the prepared baking sheets, making sure to leave 1½ to 2 inches (4 to 5 cm) between each one.

6. Bake for 11 to 14 minutes, or until the tops of the cookies are set. Remove from the oven, and allow the cookies to cool completely on the baking sheets.

7. Store the cookies in an airtight container at room temperature for up to 5 days.

THICK CHOCOLATE PEANUT BUTTER CHIP COOKIES

YIELD: 14 or 15 cookies

TOTAL TIME: 45 minutes

NO CHILLING REQUIRED!

Whenever my husband and I travel to New York City, we always make sure to visit as many bakeries as possible. One of my favorite treats to get are the huge cookies! These thick chocolate cookies are my take on those massive bakery-style cookies.

2½ cups (315 g) all-purpose flour, spooned and leveled

⅔ cup (60 g) natural unsweetened cocoa powder

1 teaspoon baking powder

½ teaspoon baking soda

½ teaspoon salt

1 cup (2 sticks, or 230 g) cold unsalted butter, cubed into small pieces (see Pro Baking Tips)

1 cup (200 g) packed light brown sugar

½ cup (100 g) granulated sugar

2 large eggs

2 teaspoons pure vanilla extract

1 bag (10 ounces, or 283 g) peanut butter chips

1. Preheat the oven to 350°F (180°C). Line two large baking sheets with parchment paper or silicone baking mats and set aside.

2. In a large mixing bowl, sift the flour and cocoa powder together, then whisk in the baking powder, baking soda, and salt until well combined. Set aside.

3. In the bowl of a stand mixer fitted with the paddle attachment or in a large mixing bowl using a handheld mixer, beat the cold cubed butter, brown sugar, and granulated sugar together for 2 to 3 minutes, or until well combined.

4. Mix in the eggs, one at a time, then mix in the vanilla extract until fully combined, making sure to stop and scrape down the sides of the bowl as needed.

5. Mix in the dry ingredients until just combined, then mix in the peanut butter chips on low speed until fully incorporated.

6. Using a ⅓-cup (3 ounces, or 85 g) measuring cup, measure out the balls of cookie dough, roll into balls, and place onto the prepared baking sheets, making sure to leave 1½ to 2 inches (4 to 5 cm) between each one.

7. Bake for 15 to 20 minutes, or until the tops of the cookies are set. Remove from the oven, and allow the cookies to cool on the baking sheets for 10 to 15 minutes, then carefully transfer the cookies to a wire rack to cool completely.

8. Store the cookies in an airtight container at room temperature for up to 1 week.

PRO BAKING TIPS

✳ You can easily cut this recipe in half to make just 7 or 8 large cookies.

✳ Unlike most of the other cookie recipes, you will be using cold butter to ensure that these cookies are nice and thick. I recommend cubing the butter into smaller pieces so that it's easier to mix together with the brown sugar and granulated sugar.

CHOCOLATE CUTOUT SUGAR COOKIES

YIELD: 25 to 30 cookies

TOTAL TIME: 2 hours 43 minutes
   (includes 1 hour of chilling time)

If you ever find yourself looking for an alternative to a traditional cutout sugar cookie, this recipe is a fantastic option! These cookies are not only soft and chocolatey, but they hold their shape extremely well after they are baked.

2¼ cups (280 g) all-purpose flour, spooned and leveled

½ cup (45 g) natural unsweetened cocoa powder

1 teaspoon baking powder

½ teaspoon salt

1 cup (2 sticks, or 230 g) unsalted butter, softened

1 cup plus 2 tablespoons (225 g) granulated sugar

1 large egg, at room temperature

1½ teaspoons pure vanilla extract

1 batch Easy Sugar Cookie Icing (page 166)

Sanding sugar, for topping (optional)

PRO BAKING TIP

To roll out the dough to an even thickness, I recommend placing a ¼-inch-thick (6 mm) square dowel on each side of the dough, then rolling it out with a rolling pin going over the dowels.

1. In a large mixing bowl, sift the flour and cocoa powder together, then whisk in the baking powder and salt until well combined. Set aside.

2. In the bowl of a stand mixer fitted with the paddle attachment or in a large mixing bowl using a handheld mixer, beat the butter and granulated sugar together for 1 to 2 minutes, or until well combined.

3. Mix in the egg and vanilla extract until fully combined, making sure to stop and scrape down the sides of the bowl as needed.

4. Mix in the dry ingredients until just combined.

5. Divide the dough in half. Lightly flour a piece of parchment paper, add half of the dough, flour the top of the dough, and then top with another piece of parchment paper. Roll out the dough between the pieces of parchment paper to ¼ inch (6 mm) thick with a rolling pin. Repeat with the other half of the dough between two additional pieces of parchment paper.

6. Leaving the sheets of dough between the parchment paper, place them on a baking sheet, and refrigerate for 1 hour.

7. Preheat the oven to 350°F (180°C). Line large baking sheets with parchment paper or silicone baking mats and set aside.

8. Remove one sheet of cookie dough from the refrigerator, and peel off the top layer of parchment paper. Using 2½- to 3-inch (6 to 7.5 cm) cookie cutters, cut the cookie dough into shapes, and place them onto the prepared baking sheets, making sure to leave 1½ to 2 inches (4 to 5 cm) between each one.

9. Roll any scrap pieces of dough between the two pieces of parchment paper, and continue cutting out shapes. Repeat with the other sheet of chilled cookie dough.

10. Bake for 11 to 13 minutes, or until the tops of the cookies are set. Remove from the oven, and allow the cookies to cool on the baking sheets for 10 minutes, then carefully transfer the cookies to a wire rack to cool completely.

11. Decorate the cooled sugar cookies with the icing and sprinkle with sanding sugar (if using). Place the cookies in a single layer in airtight containers, and allow the icing to harden fully for 20 to 24 hours. Then stack and store the cookies in an airtight container at room temperature for up to 1 week.

TURTLE COOKIE CUPS

YIELD: 24 cookie cups

TOTAL TIME: 1 hour 13 minutes

NO CHILLING REQUIRED!

There's something so delicious about the combination of crunchy pecans, gooey caramel, and chocolate. I decided to recreate that classic candy with this turtle cookie cup.

CHOCOLATE COOKIE CUPS

Nonstick cooking spray, for greasing the pan

1⅓ cups (165 g) all-purpose flour, spooned and leveled

⅓ cup (30 g) natural unsweetened cocoa powder

½ teaspoon baking soda

¼ teaspoon salt

½ cup (1 stick, or 115 g) unsalted butter, softened

½ cup (100 g) packed light brown sugar

½ cup (100 g) granulated sugar

1 large egg, at room temperature

1 teaspoon pure vanilla extract

CARAMEL FILLING AND TOPPINGS

36 soft caramel candies (300 g), unwrapped

3 tablespoons (45 ml) heavy whipping cream

24 pecan halves

2 ounces (57 g) semisweet chocolate, roughly chopped

PRO BAKING TIP

Press an indentation into the center of the cookie cups as soon as they come out of the oven.

1. **To make the chocolate cookie cups:** Preheat the oven to 350°F (180°C). Spray a 24-count mini muffin pan with nonstick cooking spray and set aside.

2. In a large mixing bowl, sift the flour and cocoa powder together, then whisk in the baking soda and salt until well combined. Set aside.

3. In the bowl of a stand mixer fitted with the paddle attachment or in a large mixing bowl using a handheld mixer, beat the butter, brown sugar, and granulated sugar together for 1 to 2 minutes, or until well combined. Mix in the egg and vanilla extract until fully combined, making sure to stop and scrape down the sides of the bowl as needed.

4. Mix in the dry ingredients until just combined.

5. Evenly distribute the cookie dough among all 24 cups in the prepared mini muffin pan, a little more than 1 tablespoon of cookie dough per cup. Press each ball of cookie dough into the cups and smooth it out.

6. Bake for 11 to 13 minutes, or until the tops of the cookie cups are set.

7. Remove from the oven, and make a deep indentation in each cookie cup using the back of a measuring teaspoon. Allow to cool completely in the muffin pan, then carefully remove the cookie cups from the pan and set aside.

8. **To make the caramel filling and assemble the cookie cups:** Add the caramel candies and heavy whipping cream to a microwave-safe bowl. Microwave in 20- to 30-second increments, making sure to stir well after each increment, until the mixture is completely melted and smooth.

9. Evenly distribute the caramel among all 24 cookie cups, filling each one almost to the top. Top each filled cookie cup with a pecan half.

10. Add the chopped chocolate to a microwave-safe bowl. Microwave in 20- to 30-second increments, making sure to stir well after each increment, until completely melted and smooth. Drizzle the melted chocolate on top of each cookie cup.

11. Store the cookie cups in an airtight container at room temperature for up to 5 days.

CHOCOLATE ORANGE COOKIES

YIELD: 18 to 20 cookies

TOTAL TIME: 1 hour 13 minutes
   (includes 30 minutes of chilling time)

My husband's grandmother, Linda, loved orange jelly sticks covered in chocolate. So much so that I knew I had to incorporate one of her favorite treats in memory of her. These chocolate cookies are infused with orange juice and zest, topped with a simple orange icing, and taste just like the orange sticks she loved so much!

CHOCOLATE ORANGE COOKIES

1⅓ cups (165 g) all-purpose flour, spooned and leveled

⅓ cup (30 g) natural unsweetened cocoa powder

½ teaspoon baking soda

¼ teaspoon salt

½ cup (1 stick, or 115 g) unsalted butter, softened

½ cup (100 g) packed light brown sugar

⅓ cup (65 g) granulated sugar

1 large egg, at room temperature

1 tablespoon (15 ml) fresh orange juice

Zest of 1 medium orange (2 teaspoons)

1 teaspoon pure vanilla extract

ORANGE ICING

1 cup (120 g) powdered sugar

2 tablespoons (30 ml) fresh orange juice, divided

1. **To make the chocolate orange cookies:** In a large mixing bowl, sift the flour and cocoa powder together, then whisk in the baking soda and salt until well combined. Set aside.

2. In the bowl of a stand mixer fitted with the paddle attachment or in a large mixing bowl using a handheld mixer, beat the butter, brown sugar, and granulated sugar together for 1 to 2 minutes, or until well combined.

3. Mix in the egg until fully combined, then mix in the 1 tablespoon orange juice, orange zest, and vanilla extract until fully combined, making sure to stop and scrape down the sides of the bowl as needed.

4. Mix in the dry ingredients until just combined. Cover tightly and refrigerate for at least 30 minutes.

5. Meanwhile, preheat the oven to 350°F (180°C). Line two large baking sheets with parchment paper or silicone baking mats and set aside.

6. Using a 1½-tablespoon cookie scoop, scoop the cookie dough onto the prepared baking sheets, making sure to leave 1½ to 2 inches (4 to 5 cm) between each one.

7. Bake for 11 to 13 minutes, or until the tops of the cookies are set. Remove from the oven, and allow the cookies to cool on the baking sheets for 5 to 10 minutes, then carefully transfer the cookies to a wire rack to cool completely.

8. **To make the orange icing:** Whisk together the powdered sugar and 1 tablespoon (15 ml) of the orange juice in a large mixing bowl until well combined; the mixture will be very thick. Add ½ teaspoon of the remaining orange juice at a time until the icing reaches your desired consistency and no lumps remain.

9. Evenly spread the icing on top of all the cooled cookies. Top with additional orange zest if desired.

10. Store the cookies in an airtight container at room temperature for up to 5 days.

PRO BAKING TIP

It's easier to zest your orange before you cut it and juice it. If you want to get more juice out of your orange, firmly roll it with your palm on the counter before cutting into it.

CHOCOLATE WHOOPIE PIES

YIELD: 16 to 18 whoopie pies

TOTAL TIME: 58 minutes

NO CHILLING REQUIRED!

These whoopie pies feature a cakey cookie base that sandwiches a delicious vanilla buttercream frosting. It's almost like biting into a slice of chocolate cake!

CHOCOLATE WHOOPIE PIES

2 cups (250 g) all-purpose flour, spooned and leveled

½ cup (45 g) natural unsweetened cocoa powder

1 teaspoon baking soda

½ teaspoon instant espresso powder (optional)

½ teaspoon salt

½ cup (1 stick, or 115 g) unsalted butter, softened

1 cup (200 g) packed light brown sugar

1 large egg, at room temperature

1½ teaspoons pure vanilla extract

1 cup (240 ml) buttermilk, at room temperature

VANILLA BUTTERCREAM FROSTING

¾ cup (170 g) unsalted butter, softened

2¼ cups (270 g) powdered sugar

3 tablespoons (45 ml) heavy whipping cream

1½ teaspoons pure vanilla extract

PRO BAKING TIP

I like to use the back of a spoon to smooth out the batter for each whoopie pie before placing them in the oven.

1. **To make the chocolate whoopie pies:** Preheat the oven to 350°F (180°C). Line large baking sheets with parchment paper or silicone baking mats and set aside.

2. In a large mixing bowl, sift the flour and cocoa powder together, then whisk in the baking soda, espresso powder (if using), and salt. Set aside.

3. In the bowl of a stand mixer fitted with the paddle attachment or in a large mixing bowl using a handheld mixer, beat the butter and brown sugar together for 1 to 2 minutes, or until well combined.

4. Mix in the egg and vanilla extract until fully combined, making sure to stop and scrape down the sides of the bowl as needed.

5. Starting and ending with the dry ingredients, mix in the dry ingredients in 3 additions, alternating with the buttermilk. Make sure to mix in each addition until just combined, and be careful not to overmix the batter.

6. Using a 1½-tablespoon cookie scoop, scoop the cookie dough onto the prepared baking sheets, making sure to leave 1½ to 2 inches (4 to 5 cm) between each one.

7. Bake for 11 to 13 minutes, or until the tops of the cookies are set and spring back when touched lightly. Remove from the oven, and allow the cookies to cool on the baking sheets for 10 minutes, then carefully transfer the cookies to a wire rack to cool completely.

8. **To make the vanilla buttercream frosting:** In the bowl of a stand mixer fitted with the paddle or whisk attachment or in a large mixing bowl using a handheld mixer, beat the butter for 1 to 2 minutes, or until smooth. Add the powdered sugar, ½ cup (60 g) at a time, mixing in each addition until well combined, then mix in the last ¼ cup (30 g) of powdered sugar until fully combined.

9. Add the heavy whipping cream and vanilla extract and continue mixing until well combined.

10. Once the cookies have cooled completely, pipe the frosting on the flat side of half of the cookies, then top with the other half of the cookies.

11. Store the cookies in an airtight container in the refrigerator for up to 4 days, and bring to room temperature before serving.

SMALL-BATCH DOUBLE CHOCOLATE CHIP COOKIES

YIELD: 8 cookies

TOTAL TIME: 27 minutes

NO CHILLING REQUIRED!

I couldn't miss the opportunity to include one more small-batch cookie in this book. This scaled-down recipe tastes just like classic chocolate cookies but makes only eight cookies!

¼ cup plus 2 tablespoons (50 g) all-purpose flour, spooned and leveled

2 tablespoons (10 g) natural unsweetened cocoa powder, sifted

¼ teaspoon baking soda

⅛ teaspoon salt

3 tablespoons (45 g) unsalted butter, softened

3 tablespoons (40 g) packed light brown sugar

2 tablespoons (25 g) granulated sugar

1 large egg yolk, at room temperature

¼ teaspoon pure vanilla extract

⅓ cup (65 g) semisweet chocolate chips

PRO BAKING TIP

Feel free to swap out the semisweet chocolate chips for any mix-in you prefer. Some other great options are peanut butter chips, white chocolate chips, M&M's, or chopped walnuts.

1. Preheat the oven to 350°F (180°C). Line a large baking sheet with parchment paper or a silicone baking mat and set aside.

2. In a large mixing bowl, sift the flour and cocoa powder together, then whisk in the baking soda and salt until well combined. Set aside.

3. In a medium mixing bowl using a handheld mixer, beat the butter, brown sugar, and granulated sugar together for 1 to 2 minutes, or until well combined.

4. Mix in the egg yolk and vanilla extract until fully combined, making sure to stop and scrape down the sides of the bowl as needed.

5. Mix in the dry ingredients until just combined, then mix in the chocolate chips on low speed until fully incorporated.

6. Using a 1½-tablespoon cookie scoop, scoop the cookie dough, roll it into a ball, and place it onto the prepared baking sheets, making sure to leave 1½ to 2 inches (4 to 5 cm) between each one.

7. Bake for 10 to 12 minutes, or until the tops of the cookies are set and start to crack. Remove from the oven, and allow the cookies to cool on the baking sheet for 5 to 10 minutes, then carefully transfer the cookies to a wire rack to cool completely.

8. Store the cookies in an airtight container at room temperature for up to 1 week.

FUN FLAVOR COMBINATIONS

Now that we've covered all the classic flavors, it's time for some fun flavor combinations!

In this chapter you will find a mix of fruity, chocolaty, caramelly, and everything in between. From maple and cinnamon to coconut and brown butter cookies, there is something for everyone.

If you are looking for a fun treat to make with your kids or just something unique and delicious, then be sure to slow down and enjoy the following recipes!

ICED LEMON POPPY SEED COOKIES

YIELD: 18 cookies

TOTAL TIME: 1 hour 12 minutes
    (includes 30 minutes of chilling time)

If you love lemon desserts as much as I do, you are going to adore these soft lemon cookies filled with poppy seeds. I highly recommend adding the two-ingredient lemon icing for even more flavor!

LEMON COOKIES

1¾ cups (220 g) all-purpose flour, spooned and leveled

1 tablespoon (8 g) poppy seeds

½ teaspoon baking soda

¼ teaspoon salt

½ cup (1 stick, or 115 g) unsalted butter, softened

¾ cup (150 g) granulated sugar

1 large egg, at room temperature

Zest of 1 medium lemon

1 tablespoon (15 ml) fresh lemon juice

1 teaspoon lemon extract

2 or 3 drops yellow liquid food coloring (optional)

LEMON ICING

1 cup (120 g) powdered sugar

2 tablespoons (30 ml) fresh lemon juice, divided

PRO BAKING TIP

It's easier to zest your lemon (avoiding the pith) before you cut it and juice it. If you want to get more juice out of your lemon, firmly roll it with your palm on the counter before cutting into it.

---

1. **To make the lemon cookies:** In a large mixing bowl, whisk together the all-purpose flour, poppy seeds, baking soda, and salt. Set aside.

2. In the bowl of a stand mixer fitted with the paddle attachment or in a large mixing bowl using a handheld mixer, beat the butter and granulated sugar together for 1 to 2 minutes, or until well combined.

3. Add the egg and mix until well combined, then mix in the lemon zest, lemon juice, lemon extract, and yellow food coloring (if using) until fully combined, making sure to stop and scrape down the sides of the bowl as needed.

4. Mix in the dry ingredients until just combined.

5. Cover tightly and refrigerate for at least 30 minutes.

6. Meanwhile, preheat the oven to 350°F (180°C). Line two large baking sheets with parchment paper or silicone baking mats and set aside.

7. Using a 1½-tablespoon cookie scoop, scoop the cookie dough onto the prepared baking sheets, making sure to leave 1½ to 2 inches (4 to 5 cm) between each one.

8. Bake for 10 to 12 minutes, or until the tops of the cookies are set. Remove from the oven, and allow the cookies to cool on the baking sheets for 5 to 10 minutes, then carefully transfer the cookies to a wire rack to cool completely.

9. **To make the lemon icing:** Whisk together the powdered sugar and 1 tablespoon (15 ml) of the lemon juice in a large mixing bowl until well combined; the mixture will be very thick.

10. Add ½ teaspoon of the remaining lemon juice at a time until the icing reaches your desired consistency and no lumps remain.

11. Evenly spread the icing on top of all the cooled cookies.

12. Store the cookies in an airtight container at room temperature for up to 5 days.

S'MORES COOKIES

YIELD: 40 to 42 cookies

TOTAL TIME: 1 hour 43 minutes
(includes 1 hour of chilling time)

Love s'mores? These cookies are made with graham cracker crumbs, filled with melty chocolate chips, and topped with toasted marshmallows. The perfect gooey treat when you are craving s'mores and a cookie!

2¼ cups (280 g) all-purpose flour, spooned and leveled

¾ cup (90 g) graham cracker crumbs (see Pro Baking Tips)

1 teaspoon baking soda

1 teaspoon salt

1 cup (2 sticks, or 230 g) unsalted butter, softened

1 cup (200 g) packed light brown sugar

⅓ cup (65 g) granulated sugar

2 large eggs, at room temperature

2 teaspoons pure vanilla extract

1 bag (12 ounces, or 340 g) semisweet chocolate chips

1½ cups (70 g) mini marshmallows

1. In a large mixing bowl, whisk together the flour, graham cracker crumbs, baking soda, and salt until well combined. Set aside.

2. In the bowl of a stand mixer fitted with the paddle attachment or in a large mixing bowl using a handheld mixer, beat the butter, brown sugar, and granulated sugar together for 1 to 2 minutes, or until well combined.

3. Mix in the eggs, one at a time, then mix in the vanilla extract, making sure to stop and scrape down the sides of the bowl as needed.

4. Mix in the dry ingredients until just combined, then mix in the chocolate chips on low speed until fully incorporated.

5. Cover tightly and refrigerate for at least 1 hour.

6. Preheat the oven to 350°F (180°C). Line large baking sheets with parchment paper or silicone baking mats and set aside.

7. Using a 1½-tablespoon cookie scoop, scoop the cookie dough onto the prepared baking sheets, making sure to leave 1½ to 2 inches (4 to 5 cm) between each one.

8. Bake for 9 to 11 minutes, or until the tops of the cookies are just set. Remove from the oven, and press three mini marshmallows into the top of each cookie. Return to the oven and bake for an additional 2 minutes. Remove from the oven, and allow the cookies to cool on the baking sheets for 10 minutes, then carefully transfer the cookies to a wire rack to cool completely.

9. Store the cookies in an airtight container at room temperature for up to 5 days.

PRO BAKING TIPS

✴ You will need about 6 full sheets of graham crackers to get ¾ cup (90 g) of graham cracker crumbs. If you want to make this recipe even easier, you can also use store-bought graham cracker crumbs.

✴ You can add the graham crackers to a food processor or blender and process until you have fine crumbs. Alternatively, you can add them to a resealable plastic bag and crush them into fine crumbs.

COOKIES AND CREAM COOKIES

YIELD: 40 to 42 cookies

TOTAL TIME: 47 minutes

NO CHILLING REQUIRED!

Because the only thing better than a cookie is a cookie with more cookies in it! Just don't forget to crush up a few more Oreos and add them on top.

2¾ cups (345 g) all-purpose flour, spooned and leveled

1 teaspoon baking soda

¾ teaspoon salt

¾ cup (1½ sticks, or 170 g) unsalted butter, softened

3 ounces (85 g) brick-style cream cheese, softened

⅔ cup (135 g) granulated sugar

½ cup (100 g) packed light brown sugar

1 large egg, at room temperature

2 teaspoons pure vanilla extract

1 cup (190 g) white chocolate chips

12 Oreos, chopped into small pieces

PRO BAKING TIP

I like to chop up 5 or 6 extra Oreos and gently press a few pieces into the tops of each cookie before baking them.

1. Preheat the oven to 350°F (180°C). Line large baking sheets with parchment paper or silicone baking mats and set aside.

2. In a large mixing bowl, whisk together the flour, baking soda, and salt until well combined. Set aside.

3. In the bowl of a stand mixer fitted with the paddle attachment or in a large mixing bowl using a handheld mixer, beat the butter and cream cheese together until well combined. Mix in the granulated sugar and brown sugar for 1 to 2 minutes, or until well combined.

4. Mix in the egg and vanilla extract, making sure to stop and scrape down the sides of the bowl as needed.

5. Mix in the dry ingredients until just combined, then gently fold in the white chocolate chips and chopped Oreos.

6. Using a 1½-tablespoon cookie scoop, scoop the cookie dough onto the prepared baking sheets, making sure to leave 1½ to 2 inches (4 to 5 cm) between each one. Gently press each ball of cookie dough down to slightly flatten it.

7. Bake for 9 to 12 minutes, or until the tops of the cookies are set. Remove from the oven, and allow the cookies to cool on the baking sheets for 5 to 10 minutes, then carefully transfer the cookies to a wire rack to cool completely.

8. Store the cookies in an airtight container at room temperature for up to 1 week.

TOASTED COCONUT SNOWBALL COOKIES

YIELD: 36 to 38 cookies

TOTAL TIME: 49 minutes

NO CHILLING REQUIRED!

These delicious snowball cookies are packed with coconut flavor from the combination of coconut extract and toasted coconut. They're sure to delight any coconut lover!

1 cup (70 g) sweetened shredded coconut

1 cup (2 sticks, or 230 g) unsalted butter, softened

1½ cups (180 g) powdered sugar, divided

1 teaspoon coconut extract

1 teaspoon pure vanilla extract

2¼ cups (280 g) all-purpose flour, spooned and leveled

¼ teaspoon salt

PRO BAKING TIP

Make sure to keep a close eye on the coconut as it's toasting in the oven. It can go from lightly browned to burnt in a matter of seconds.

1. Preheat the oven to 350°F (180°C). Line a large baking sheet with parchment paper or a silicone baking mat. Spread the coconut on the baking sheet and bake for 6 to 10 minutes, stirring well every 1 to 2 minutes, until the coconut is lightly browned. Remove the coconut from the oven, and set aside to cool completely.

2. Line two more large baking sheets with parchment paper or silicone baking mats and set aside.

3. In the bowl of a stand mixer fitted with the paddle attachment or in a large mixing bowl using a handheld mixer, beat the butter and ½ cup (60 g) of powdered sugar together for 1 to 2 minutes, or until well combined.

4. Mix in the coconut extract and vanilla extract until fully combined, making sure to stop and scrape down the sides of the bowl as needed.

5. Mix in the flour and salt until just combined, then gently fold in the toasted coconut until fully incorporated.

6. Using a 1-tablespoon cookie scoop, scoop the cookie dough onto the prepared baking sheets, making sure to leave 1½ to 2 inches (4 to 5 cm) between each one.

7. Bake for 12 to 14 minutes, or until the tops of the cookies are set. Remove from the oven, and allow the cookies to cool on the baking sheets for 5 to 10 minutes.

8. While the cookies are still warm, roll each one in the remaining 1 cup (120 g) powdered sugar. Allow to cool completely, then roll all the cookies one more time in the powdered sugar.

9. Store the cookies in an airtight container at room temperature for up to 1 week.

BROOKIES

YIELD: 48 cookies

TOTAL TIME: 2 hours
  (includes 50 minutes of chilling time)

No one should ever have to face the difficult decision of choosing between brownies and cookies. With these homemade brookies, you don't have to decide! This delicious cookie recipe fuses together two different types of cookie dough—chocolate chip and brownie—to create one seriously delicious treat.

BROWNIE COOKIE DOUGH

1 cup (125 g) all-purpose flour, spooned and leveled

¼ cup (22 g) natural unsweetened cocoa powder

1 teaspoon baking powder

¼ teaspoon salt

6 tablespoons (85 g) unsalted butter, sliced into tablespoon-size pieces

1¼ cups (8 ounces, or 226 g) semisweet chocolate chips

¾ cup (150 g) packed light brown sugar

½ cup (100 g) granulated sugar

2 large eggs, at room temperature

1 teaspoon pure vanilla extract

1. **To make the brownie cookie dough:** In a large mixing bowl, sift the flour and cocoa powder together, then whisk in the baking powder and salt until well combined. Set aside.

2. Add the sliced butter and semisweet chocolate chips to a large microwave-safe bowl. Microwave in 30-second increments, stirring well after each increment, until the mixture is completely melted and smooth. Whisk or stir in the brown sugar and granulated sugar until fully combined.

3. Mix in the eggs and vanilla extract, making sure to stop and scrape down the sides of the bowl as needed.

4. Mix in the dry ingredients until just combined.

5. Cover tightly and refrigerate for 15 to 20 minutes while you prepare the chocolate chip cookie dough.

6. **To make the chocolate chip cookie dough:** In a large mixing bowl, whisk together the flour, baking soda, and salt until well combined. Set aside.

7. In the bowl of a stand mixer fitted with the paddle attachment or in a large mixing bowl using a handheld mixer, beat the butter, brown sugar, and granulated sugar together for 1 to 2 minutes, or until well combined.

8. Mix in the egg, egg yolk, and vanilla extract, making sure to stop and scrape down the sides of the bowl as needed.

9. Mix in the dry ingredients until just combined, then mix in the chocolate chips on low speed until fully incorporated.

10. Line two large baking sheets with parchment paper or silicone baking mats.

11. Using a 1-tablespoon cookie scoop, scoop the chocolate chip cookie dough onto the prepared baking sheets, leaving some space for the brownie cookie dough.

12. Remove the brownie cookie dough from the refrigerator. Using a 1-tablespoon cookie scoop, scoop the brownie cookie dough onto the prepared baking sheets, next to the chocolate chip cookie dough.

continued

CHOCOLATE CHIP COOKIE DOUGH

2 cups plus 2 tablespoons (265 g) all-purpose flour, spooned and leveled

¾ teaspoon baking soda

¾ teaspoon salt

¾ cup (1½ sticks, or 170 g) unsalted butter, softened

¾ cup (150 g) packed light brown sugar

⅓ cup (65 g) granulated sugar

1 large egg, at room temperature

1 large egg yolk, at room temperature

1½ teaspoons pure vanilla extract

1¼ cups (8 ounces, or 226 g) semisweet chocolate chips

PRO BAKING TIP

I like to press a few chocolate chips into the chocolate chip cookie side soon after the cookies come out of the oven. This is optional, but makes them look prettier.

13. Push 1 ball of the chocolate chip cookie dough and 1 ball of the brownie cookie dough together (see the photo below for reference). Repeat with the remaining balls of cookie dough.

14. Cover the baking sheets tightly with plastic wrap, and return to the refrigerator to chill for at least 30 minutes.

15. Meanwhile, preheat the oven to 350°F (180°C). Line two more large baking sheets with parchment paper or silicone baking mats and set aside.

16. Remove the cookie dough from the refrigerator, and divide the dough evenly between the baking sheets, making sure to leave a little room between each dough ball.

17. Bake for 12 to 14 minutes, or until the tops of the cookies are set. Remove from the oven, and allow the cookies to cool on the baking sheets for 10 minutes, then carefully transfer the cookies to a wire rack to cool completely.

18. Store the cookies in an airtight container at room temperature for up to 1 week.

BROWN BUTTER BUTTERSCOTCH OATMEAL COOKIES

YIELD: 22 cookies

TOTAL TIME: 2 hours 53 minutes
   (includes 2 hours of chilling time)

If you have never tried browning your butter, then these cookies are a great starting point! Brown butter has a deep, rich, nutty flavor that pairs perfectly with the oats and butterscotch chips in these cookies. Don't forget the pinch of sea salt on top too—it's the final touch that really makes this recipe.

½ cup (1 stick, or 115 g) unsalted butter, sliced into tablespoon-size pieces

¾ cup (95 g) all-purpose flour, spooned and leveled

½ teaspoon baking soda

½ teaspoon ground cinnamon

¼ teaspoon salt

1¼ cups (125 g) old-fashioned rolled oats

¾ cup (150 g) packed light brown sugar

1 large egg, at room temperature

1 teaspoon pure vanilla extract

¾ cup (140 g) butterscotch chips

Sea salt, for topping (optional)

1. To brown the butter, add the sliced butter to a skillet or saucepan. Place over medium heat until the butter is completely melted, then allow it to cook, stirring or swirling the pan often, for an additional 5 to 7 minutes, or until the butter is browned. The butter is browned once you see brown bits of milk solids on the bottom of the pan and smell a nutty aroma (see the photo on page 121 for reference). Immediately remove the butter from the heat and pour it into a heatproof dish. Place in the refrigerator uncovered for 1 hour, or until the butter is solidified.

2. In a large mixing bowl, whisk together the flour, baking soda, ground cinnamon, and salt until well combined. Stir in the old-fashioned rolled oats and set aside.

3. In the bowl of a stand mixer fitted with the paddle attachment or in a large mixing bowl using a handheld mixer, beat the chilled brown butter and brown sugar together for 1 to 2 minutes, or until well combined.

4. Mix in the egg and vanilla extract until fully combined, making sure to stop and scrape down the sides of the bowl as needed.

5. Mix in the dry ingredients until just combined, then mix in the butterscotch chips on low speed until fully incorporated.

6. Cover tightly and refrigerate for at least 1 hour.

7. Preheat the oven to 350°F (180°C). Line two large baking sheets with parchment paper or silicone baking mats and set aside.

8. Using a 1½-tablespoon cookie scoop, scoop the cookie dough onto the prepared baking sheets, making sure to leave 1½ to 2 inches (4 to 5 cm) between each one.

9. Bake for 11 to 13 minutes, or until the tops of the cookies are set and the edges are lightly browned. Remove from the oven, and allow the cookies to cool on the baking sheets for 5 to 10 minutes, then carefully transfer the cookies to a wire rack to cool completely. Sprinkle each cookie with a little sea salt (if using).

10. Store the cookies in an airtight container at room temperature for up to 1 week.

continued

PRO BAKING TIPS

✳ I recommend using a light-colored skillet or saucepan to brown your butter. It will make it much easier to tell when the butter is ready to be removed from the heat.

✳ When browning butter, it's best to use butter sliced into tablespoon-size pieces so that it melts evenly.

✳ As soon as you see brown bits on the bottom of your pan and smell a nutty aroma, remove the butter from the heat and pour it into a heatproof dish. This will stop the cooking and prevent the butter from burning.

BUTTER PECAN COOKIES

YIELD: 40 to 42 cookies

TOTAL TIME: 2 hours 52 minutes
  (includes 2 hours of chilling time)

These cookies are soft, buttery, and chock-full of toasted pecans and toffee bits. I think they would even be fantastic with a little bit of vanilla ice cream sandwiched between them!

1½ cups (180 g) chopped pecans

2¾ cups (345 g) all-purpose flour, spooned and leveled

1 teaspoon baking soda

½ teaspoon ground cinnamon

1 teaspoon salt

1 cup (2 sticks, or 230 g) unsalted butter, softened

1 cup (200 g) packed light brown sugar

½ cup (100 g) granulated sugar

2 large eggs, at room temperature

2 teaspoons pure vanilla extract

¾ cup (120 g) toffee bits

PRO BAKING TIP

It's best to toast the pecans first so that they have time to cool before you add them to the cookie dough.

1. Preheat the oven to 350°F (180°C). Spread the chopped pecans in a single layer on a large baking sheet lined with parchment paper or a silicone baking mat. Bake for 7 to 10 minutes, stirring a couple of times to ensure that the pecans bake evenly. Remove from the oven, and set aside to cool completely.

2. In a large mixing bowl, whisk together the flour, baking soda, ground cinnamon, and salt until well combined. Set aside.

3. In the bowl of a stand mixer fitted with the paddle attachment or in a large mixing bowl using a handheld mixer, beat the butter, brown sugar, and granulated sugar together for 1 to 2 minutes, or until well combined.

4. Mix in the eggs, one at a time, then mix in the vanilla extract until fully combined, making sure to stop and scrape down the sides of the bowl as needed.

5. Mix in the dry ingredients until just combined, then mix in the chopped pecans and toffee bits on low speed until fully incorporated.

6. Cover tightly and refrigerate for at least 2 hours.

7. Preheat the oven to 350°F (180°C). Line large baking sheets with parchment paper or silicone baking mats and set aside.

8. Using a 1½-tablespoon cookie scoop, scoop the cookie dough onto the prepared baking sheets, making sure to leave 1½ to 2 inches (4 to 5 cm) between each one.

9. Bake for 9 to 12 minutes, or until the tops of the cookies are set and the edges are lightly browned. Remove from the oven, and allow the cookies to cool on the baking sheets for 5 to 10 minutes, then carefully transfer the cookies to a wire rack to cool completely.

10. Store the cookies in an airtight container at room temperature for up to 1 week.

ICED MAPLE CINNAMON COOKIES

YIELD: 20 to 22 cookies

TOTAL TIME: 1 hour 51 minutes
(includes 1 hour of chilling time)

These cookies are arguably my favorite recipe in this cookbook—and that's saying a lot! They are made with real maple syrup and ground cinnamon, then topped with a maple cinnamon icing.

MAPLE CINNAMON COOKIES

2 cups (250 g) all-purpose flour, spooned and leveled

1 teaspoon ground cinnamon

½ teaspoon baking soda

¼ teaspoon salt

½ cup (1 stick, or 115 g) unsalted butter, softened

¾ cup (150 g) packed light brown sugar

3 tablespoons (45 ml) pure maple syrup

1 large egg, at room temperature

1 teaspoon pure vanilla extract

½ teaspoon maple extract

MAPLE CINNAMON ICING

1¼ cups (150 g) powdered sugar

¼ teaspoon ground cinnamon

2 tablespoons (30 ml) pure maple syrup

2 tablespoons (30 ml) whole milk, divided

PRO BAKING TIP
I recommend using pure maple syrup in these cookies for the best flavor.

1. **To make the maple cinnamon cookies:** In a large mixing bowl, whisk together the flour, ground cinnamon, baking soda, and salt. Set aside.

2. In the bowl of a stand mixer fitted with the paddle attachment or in a large mixing bowl using a handheld mixer, beat the butter and brown sugar together for 1 to 2 minutes, or until well combined.

3. Mix in the maple syrup, egg, vanilla extract, and maple extract until fully combined, making sure to stop and scrape down the sides of the bowl as needed.

4. Mix in the dry ingredients until just combined.

5. Cover tightly and refrigerate for at least 1 hour.

6. Preheat the oven to 350°F (180°C). Line two large baking sheets with parchment paper or silicone baking mats and set aside.

7. Using a 1½-tablespoon cookie scoop, scoop the cookie dough onto the prepared baking sheets, making sure to leave 1½ to 2 inches (4 to 5 cm) between each one.

8. Bake for 9 to 11 minutes, or until the tops of the cookie are set. Remove from the oven, and allow the cookies to cool on the baking sheets for 5 to 10 minutes, then carefully transfer the cookies to a wire rack to cool completely.

9. **To make the maple cinnamon icing:** Whisk together the powdered sugar, ground cinnamon, maple syrup, and 1 tablespoon (15 ml) of the milk in a large mixing bowl until well combined; the mixture will be very thick.

10. Add ½ teaspoon of the remaining milk at a time until the icing reaches your desired consistency and no lumps remain.

11. Evenly spread the icing on top of all the cooled cookies.

12. Store the cookies in an airtight container at room temperature for up to 5 days.

STRAWBERRY SHORTCAKE COOKIES

YIELD: 26 to 28 cookies

TOTAL TIME: 1 hour

NO CHILLING REQUIRED!

These cookies not only incorporate chopped strawberries but also a delicious vanilla icing that takes them over the top. It's like biting into a mini strawberry shortcake, but it's much easier to make!

STRAWBERRY SHORTCAKE COOKIES

2 cups (250 g) all-purpose flour, spooned and leveled

⅔ cup (135 g) granulated sugar

2 teaspoons baking powder

¼ teaspoon salt

6 tablespoons (85 g) cold unsalted butter, cubed into small pieces (see Pro Baking Tip)

½ cup (120 ml) cold heavy whipping cream

1 large egg

1 teaspoon pure vanilla extract

1¼ cups (180 g) chopped strawberries

VANILLA ICING

1½ cups (180 g) powdered sugar

2 tablespoons (30 ml) whole milk, plus more if needed

½ teaspoon pure vanilla extract

1. **To make the strawberry shortcake cookies:** Preheat the oven to 375°F (190°C). Line two large baking sheets with parchment paper or silicone baking mats and set aside.

2. In a large mixing bowl, whisk together the flour, granulated sugar, baking powder, and salt until well combined. Add the cubed cold butter, and cut it into the dry ingredients with a pastry cutter or fork until you have small pea-size crumbs. Set aside.

3. In a separate mixing bowl, whisk together the heavy whipping cream, egg, and vanilla extract until fully combined.

4. Pour the wet ingredients into the dry ingredients, and gently mix until the dough starts to come together. Gently fold in the chopped strawberries until fully incorporated.

5. Using a 1½-tablespoon cookie scoop, scoop the cookie dough onto the prepared baking sheets, making sure to leave 1½ to 2 inches (4 to 5 cm) between each one.

6. Bake for 12 to 14 minutes, or until the tops of the cookies are set. Remove from the oven, and allow the cookies to cool on the baking sheets for 10 minutes, then carefully transfer the cookies to a wire rack to cool completely.

7. **To make the vanilla icing:** Whisk together the powdered sugar, milk, and vanilla extract in a large mixing bowl until well combined and no lumps remain. If needed, mix in an additional ½ teaspoon of milk at a time until the icing reaches your desired consistency.

8. Drizzle the icing on top of all the cooled cookies.

9. Store the cookies in an airtight container at room temperature for up to 3 days.

PRO BAKING TIP

The butter in this dough needs to be cold when the cookies go into the oven so that it can melt and create steam pockets, resulting in a light, tender texture. If the butter is a bit warm, place the baking sheets with the balls of cookie dough in the freezer for 5 to 10 minutes, and then bake the cookies as directed.

BLUEBERRY MUFFIN-TOP COOKIES

YIELD: 36 cookies

TOTAL TIME: 1 hour

NO CHILLING REQUIRED!

These cookies are a throwback to a treat that my husband, Josh, and I always used to get back in college: blueberry muffin tops! It's just like eating the best part of a muffin.

BLUEBERRY MUFFIN-TOP COOKIES

2¼ cups (280 g) all-purpose flour, spooned and leveled

2 teaspoons baking powder

½ teaspoon salt

¾ cup (1½ sticks, or 170 g) unsalted butter, softened

¾ cup (150 g) packed light brown sugar

⅓ cup (65 g) granulated sugar

1 large egg, at room temperature

1½ teaspoons pure vanilla extract

½ cup (120 g) sour cream, at room temperature

1½ cups (225 g) fresh blueberries

VANILLA ICING

1½ cups (180 g) powdered sugar

2 tablespoons (30 ml) whole milk, plus more if needed

½ teaspoon pure vanilla extract

PRO BAKING TIP

If you want to try a different icing on these cookies, use the lemon icing from the Iced Lemon Poppy Seed Cookies (page 109).

---

1. **To make the blueberry muffin-top cookies:** Preheat the oven to 350°F (180°C). Line large baking sheets with parchment paper or silicone baking mats and set aside.

2. In a large mixing bowl, whisk together the flour, baking powder, and salt until well combined. Set aside.

3. In the bowl of a stand mixer fitted with the paddle attachment or in a large mixing bowl using a handheld mixer, beat the butter, brown sugar, and granulated sugar together for 1 to 2 minutes, or until well combined.

4. Mix in the egg and vanilla extract until fully combined, making sure to stop and scrape down the sides of the bowl as needed.

5. Mix in the dry ingredients in 2 additions, alternating with the sour cream. Make sure to mix in each addition until just combined, and be careful not to overmix the batter. Gently fold in the blueberries until fully incorporated.

6. Using a 1½-tablespoon cookie scoop, scoop the cookie dough onto the prepared baking sheets, making sure to leave 1½ to 2 inches (4 to 5 cm) between each one.

7. Bake for 14 to 15 minutes, or until the tops of the cookies are set. Remove from the oven, and allow the cookies to cool on the baking sheets for 10 minutes, then carefully transfer the cookies to a wire rack to cool completely.

8. **To make the vanilla icing:** Whisk together the powdered sugar, milk, and the vanilla extract in a large mixing bowl until well combined and no lumps remain. If needed, mix in an additional ½ teaspoon of milk at a time until the icing reaches your desired consistency.

9. Drizzle the icing on top of all the cooled cookies.

10. Store the cookies in an airtight container at room temperature for up to 3 days.

SALTED CARAMEL CHOCOLATE CHIP COOKIE BARS

YIELD: 24 bars

TOTAL TIME: 3 hours 45 minutes
(includes 2 hours of cooling time)

Who can say no to any dessert that has salted caramel in the name? I sure can't! These cookie bars are made with a basic chocolate chip cookie dough, and then are filled with an easy salted caramel sauce and topped with a little more sea salt for good measure.

CHOCOLATE CHIP COOKIE BARS

2½ cups (315 g) all-purpose flour, spooned and leveled

1 teaspoon baking soda

¾ teaspoon table salt

1 cup (2 sticks, or 230 g) unsalted butter, softened

1 cup (200 g) packed light brown sugar

⅓ cup (65 g) granulated sugar

2 large eggs, at room temperature

2 teaspoons pure vanilla extract

1 bag (12 ounces, or 340g) semisweet chocolate chips

Sea salt, for topping (optional)

SALTED CARAMEL SAUCE

1 bag (11 ounces, or 311 g) soft caramel candies, unwrapped

3 tablespoons (45 ml) heavy whipping cream

½ teaspoon sea salt

1. **To make the chocolate chip cookie bars:** Preheat the oven to 350°F (180°C). Line a 9 x 13-inch (23 x 33 cm) baking pan with aluminum foil or parchment paper and set aside.

2. In a large mixing bowl, whisk together the flour, baking soda, and salt until well combined. Set aside.

3. In the bowl of a stand mixer fitted with the paddle attachment or in a large mixing bowl using a handheld mixer, beat the butter, brown sugar, and granulated sugar together for 1 to 2 minutes, or until well combined.

4. Mix in the eggs, one at a time, then mix in the vanilla extract until fully combined, making sure to stop and scrape down the sides of the bowl as needed.

5. Mix in the dry ingredients until just combined, then mix in the chocolate chips on low speed until fully incorporated.

6. Scoop half of the cookie dough into the prepared baking pan and spread it into one even layer. Lift the foil or parchment paper out of the pan, place it on a baking sheet, and place the dough in the freezer to chill for at least 25 minutes.

7. Line the baking pan again with aluminum foil or parchment paper, leaving some overhang for easy removal. Press the remaining half of the cookie dough into the baking pan and spread it into one even layer.

8. Bake the bottom layer of cookie dough for 15 minutes, or until the top is just set and the edges are lightly browned. Remove from the oven and set aside.

9. **To make the salted caramel sauce:** Add the caramel candies and heavy whipping cream to a microwave-safe bowl. Microwave in 20- to 30-second increments, stirring well after each increment, until the mixture is completely melted and smooth. Stir the ½ teaspoon of sea salt into the melted caramel until well combined.

10. Pour the salted caramel sauce onto the prebaked cookie layer (see the image on page 132 for reference). Spread the caramel, leaving a ½-inch (13 mm) border.

continued

11. Remove the chilled cookie dough layer from the freezer. Peel it off the foil or parchment paper and place it on top of the caramel layer.

12. Bake for an additional 20 to 25 minutes, or until the tops of the bars are set and lightly browned.

13. Remove from the oven, and transfer the pan to a wire rack to cool completely. Once cooled, lift the bars out of the pan using the parchment paper or foil overhang, and slice into bars. Top with additional sea salt (if using).

14. Store the bars in an airtight container at room temperature for up to 5 days.

CHERRY CHEESECAKE SUGAR COOKIE CUPS

YIELD: 24 cookie cups

TOTAL TIME: 1 hour 34 minutes
    (includes 30 minutes of cooling time)

The base of these cookies features a graham cracker cookie cup, which is filled with a homemade cherry filling and topped with a no-bake cheesecake mixture. It's just like a mini cherry cheesecake in bite-size form!

CHERRY FILLING

1 cup (160 g) pitted and halved sweet
    cherries

2 tablespoons (30 ml) water

1 tablespoon (8 g) cornstarch

2 tablespoons (25 g) granulated sugar

½ teaspoon fresh lemon juice

GRAHAM CRACKER COOKIE CUPS

Nonstick cooking spray, for greasing the
    pan

1 cup plus 2 tablespoons (140 g) all-
    purpose flour, spooned and leveled

½ cup (60 g) graham cracker crumbs

½ teaspoon baking soda

¼ teaspoon salt

½ cup (1 stick, or 115 g) unsalted butter,
    softened

⅓ cup (65 g) packed light brown sugar

⅓ cup (65 g) granulated sugar

1 large egg, at room temperature

1 teaspoon pure vanilla extract

1. **To make the cherry filling:** Add the cherries, water, cornstarch, granulated sugar, and lemon juice to a large saucepan and stir until well combined.

2. Place the saucepan over medium heat and cook, stirring occasionally, for 4 to 5 minutes, or until the cherries start to soften and release their juices. Mash the cherries with a fork or potato masher to break down any large chunks. Cook for an additional 1 to 2 minutes, stirring often, until the mixture has thickened.

3. Remove from the heat and transfer the cherry filling to a heatproof bowl. Refrigerate to cool completely.

4. **To make the graham cracker cookie cups:** Preheat the oven to 350°F (180°C). Spray a 24-count mini muffin pan with nonstick cooking spray and set aside.

5. In a large mixing bowl, whisk together the flour, graham cracker crumbs, baking soda, and salt until well combined. Set aside.

6. In the bowl of a stand mixer fitted with the paddle attachment or in a large mixing bowl using a handheld mixer, beat the butter, brown sugar, and granulated sugar together for 1 to 2 minutes, or until well combined.

7. Mix in the egg and vanilla extract until fully combined, making sure to stop and scrape down the sides of the bowl as needed.

8. Mix in the dry ingredients until just combined.

9. Evenly distribute the cookie dough among all 24 cups in the mini muffin pan, a little more than 1 tablespoon of cookie dough per cup. Press each ball of cookie dough into the cups and smooth it out.

10. Bake for 10 to 12 minutes, or until the edges of the cookie cups are lightly browned and the tops are set.

continued

CHEESECAKE TOPPING

4 ounces (113 g) brick-style cream cheese, softened

⅓ cup (40 g) powdered sugar

1 teaspoon fresh lemon juice

½ teaspoon pure vanilla extract

⅓ cup (80 ml) cold heavy whipping cream

PRO BAKING TIPS

* Pit the cherries and cut them in half before measuring them.

* The cherry filling needs to cool completely before adding it to the cookie cups.

11. Remove from the oven, and make an indention in each cookie cup using the back of a measuring teaspoon. Allow to cool completely in the muffin pan, then carefully remove them from the pan and set aside.

12. **To make the cheesecake topping:** In the bowl of a stand mixer fitted with the paddle attachment or in a large mixing bowl using a handheld mixer, beat the cream cheese until smooth. Add the powdered sugar, lemon juice, and vanilla extract, and mix until fully combined, making sure to stop and scrape down the sides of the bowl as needed. Set aside.

13. In the bowl of a stand mixer fitted with the paddle attachment or in a separate large mixing bowl using a handheld mixer, mix the cold heavy whipping cream on low-medium speed for 30 seconds to 1 minute, and then increase the speed to medium-high and continue mixing until stiff peaks form.

14. Gently fold the whipped cream into the cream cheese mixture until just combined.

15. Remove the cherry filling from the refrigerator. Evenly distribute the cherry filling among all the cookie cups, filling each one just to the top.

16. Add the cheesecake topping to a piping bag with a piping tip (I used Wilton 1M), and pipe on top of the cooled cookie cups.

17. Store the cookie cups in an airtight container in the refrigerator for up to 3 days.

COOKIE BUTTER COOKIES

YIELD: 22 to 24 cookies

TOTAL TIME: 37 minutes

NO CHILLING REQUIRED!

If you don't eat peanuts, then this recipe is a great alternative to peanut butter cookies! These cookies are made with a creamy cookie butter spread and taste like a Biscoff cookie, only softer.

1⅔ cups (210 g) all-purpose flour, spooned and leveled

½ teaspoon baking soda

¼ teaspoon salt

½ cup (1 stick, or 115 g) unsalted butter, softened

½ cup (100 g) packed light brown sugar

¼ cup (50 g) granulated sugar

½ cup (145 g) cookie butter

1 large egg, at room temperature

1 teaspoon pure vanilla extract

PRO BAKING TIP

I prefer to roll each ball of dough between my hands so that they are perfectly round and bake up nice and smooth.

1. Preheat the oven to 350°F (180°C). Line two large baking sheets with parchment paper or silicone baking mats and set aside.

2. In a large mixing bowl, whisk together the flour, baking soda, and salt until well combined. Set aside.

3. In the bowl of a stand mixer fitted with the paddle attachment or in a large mixing bowl using a handheld mixer, beat the butter, brown sugar, and granulated sugar together for 1 to 2 minutes, or until well combined.

4. Mix in the cookie butter, egg, and vanilla extract until fully combined, making sure to stop and scrape down the sides of the bowl as needed.

5. Mix in the dry ingredients until just combined.

6. Using a 1½-tablespoon cookie scoop, scoop the cookie dough onto the prepared baking sheets, making sure to leave 1½ to 2 inches (4 to 5 cm) between each one.

7. Bake for 10 to 12 minutes, or until the tops of the cookies are set. Remove from the oven, and allow the cookies to cool on the baking sheets for 5 to 10 minutes, then carefully transfer the cookies to a wire rack to cool completely.

8. Store the cookies in an airtight container at room temperature for up to 1 week.

CELEBRATION COOKIES

Cookies are such a perfect treat that I absolutely love to make year-round. That's why I decided to dedicate an entire chapter to cookies for celebrating holidays, life events, and the seasons.

In the next few pages you will find cookies that are perfect for Saint Patrick's Day, Easter, Fourth of July, and more. There are even some fun birthday treats if you prefer to make something other than a traditional birthday cake.

But I couldn't stop there, so I added a few fall-inspired recipes made with pumpkin and apples too!

RED VELVET COOKIES

YIELD: 22 to 24 cookies

TOTAL TIME: 37 minutes

NO CHILLING REQUIRED!

These delicious cookies have hints of vanilla and chocolate in them and taste just like a classic red velvet cake! You can make these for Valentine's Day or Christmas.

1½ cups (190 g) all-purpose flour, spooned and leveled

2 tablespoons (10 g) natural unsweetened cocoa powder

½ teaspoon baking soda

¼ teaspoon salt

½ cup (1 stick, or 115 g) unsalted butter, softened

½ cup (100 g) packed light brown sugar

⅓ cup (65 g) granulated sugar

1 large egg, at room temperature

1 teaspoon pure vanilla extract

1 tablespoon (15 ml) red liquid food coloring

1 cup (190 g) white chocolate chips

PRO BAKING TIP
Feel free to swap out the white chocolate chips in these cookies for milk chocolate, semisweet, or even dark chocolate chips.

1. Preheat the oven to 350°F (180°C). Line two large baking sheets with parchment paper or silicone baking mats and set aside.

2. In a large mixing bowl, sift the flour and cocoa powder together, then whisk in the baking soda and salt until well combined. Set aside.

3. In the bowl of a stand mixer fitted with the paddle attachment or in a large mixing bowl using a handheld mixer, beat the butter, brown sugar, and granulated sugar together for 1 to 2 minutes, or until well combined.

4. Mix in the egg, vanilla extract, and red food coloring, making sure to stop and scrape down the sides of the bowl as needed.

5. Mix in the dry ingredients until just combined, then mix in the white chocolate chips on low speed until fully incorporated.

6. Using a 1½-tablespoon cookie scoop, scoop the cookie dough onto the prepared baking sheets, making sure to leave 1½ to 2 inches (4 to 5 cm) between each one.

7. Bake for 10 to 12 minutes, or until the tops of the cookies are set. Remove from the oven, and allow the cookies to cool on the baking sheets for 5 to 10 minutes, then carefully transfer the cookies to a wire rack to cool completely.

8. Store the cookies in an airtight container at room temperature for up to 1 week.

RED VELVET WHOOPIE PIES

YIELD: 16 whoopie pies

TOTAL TIME: 57 minutes

NO CHILLING REQUIRED!

I couldn't resist adding one more red velvet treat to this cookbook! These whoopie pies are soft and cakey with just a hint of chocolate in them.

RED VELVET COOKIES

2¼ cups (280 g) all-purpose flour, spooned and leveled

¼ cup (22 g) natural unsweetened cocoa powder

1 teaspoon baking soda

½ teaspoon salt

¾ cup (1½ sticks, or 170 g) unsalted butter, softened

1 cup (200 g) packed light brown sugar

1 large egg, at room temperature

1 teaspoon pure vanilla extract

1 tablespoon (15 ml) red liquid food coloring

¾ cup (180 ml) buttermilk, at room temperature

CREAM CHEESE FROSTING

8 ounces (226 g) brick-style cream cheese, softened

½ cup (1 stick, or 115 g) unsalted butter, softened

2 cups (240 g) powdered sugar

1 teaspoon pure vanilla extract

PRO BAKING TIP

Don't have a piping bag? Scoop the frosting into a resealable plastic bag, cut off a corner, and pipe.

1. **To make the red velvet cookies:** Preheat the oven to 350°F (180°C). Line large baking sheets with parchment paper or silicone baking mats and set aside.

2. In a large mixing bowl, sift the flour and cocoa powder together, then whisk in the baking soda and salt. Set aside.

3. In the bowl of a stand mixer fitted with the paddle attachment or in a large mixing bowl using a handheld mixer, beat the butter and brown sugar together for 1 to 2 minutes, or until well combined.

4. Mix in the egg, vanilla extract, and red food coloring until fully combined, making sure to stop and scrape down the sides of the bowl as needed.

5. Starting and ending with the dry ingredients, mix in the dry ingredients in 3 additions, alternating with the buttermilk. Make sure to mix in each addition until just combined, and be careful not to overmix the batter.

6. Using a 1½-tablespoon cookie scoop, scoop the cookie dough onto the prepared baking sheets, making sure to leave 1½ to 2 inches (4 to 5 cm) between each one.

7. Bake for 10 to 12 minutes, or until the tops of the cookies are set and spring back when touched lightly. Remove from the oven, and allow the cookies to cool on the baking sheets for 10 minutes, then carefully transfer the cookies to a wire rack to cool completely.

8. **To make the cream cheese frosting:** In the bowl of a stand mixer fitted with the whisk or paddle attachment or in a large mixing bowl using a handheld mixer, beat the cream cheese until smooth.

9. Add the butter and mix for about 30 seconds to 1 minute, or until well combined and smooth. Add the powdered sugar and vanilla extract, and continue mixing until fully combined, stopping to scrape down the sides of the bowl as needed.

10. Once the cookies have cooled completely, pipe the frosting on the flat side of half of the cookies, then top with the other half of the cookies.

11. Store the cookies in an airtight container in the refrigerator for up to 4 days.

MINT CHOCOLATE CHIP COOKIES

YIELD: 38 to 40 cookies

TOTAL TIME: 2 hours 37 minutes
(includes 2 hours of chilling time)

One of my favorite flavors of ice cream is mint chocolate chip, so I decided to recreate that classic flavor with these cookies, which are not only perfect for mint chocolate lovers but would make an adorable treat for Saint Patrick's Day or Halloween!

2¾ cups (345 g) all-purpose flour, spooned and leveled

1 teaspoon baking soda

1 teaspoon salt

1 cup (2 sticks, or 230 g) unsalted butter, softened

1 cup (200 g) packed light brown sugar

½ cup (100 g) granulated sugar

2 large eggs, at room temperature

1 teaspoon pure vanilla extract

1½ teaspoons peppermint extract

1 teaspoon green liquid food coloring

1 bag (12 ounces, or 340 g) semisweet chocolate chips

PRO BAKING TIP

I find that mint extract can be too strong, so I highly recommend using peppermint extract in these cookies.

1. In a large mixing bowl, whisk together the flour, baking soda, and salt until well combined. Set aside.

2. In the bowl of a stand mixer fitted with the paddle attachment or in a large mixing bowl using a handheld mixer, beat the butter, brown sugar, and granulated sugar together for 1 to 2 minutes, or until well combined.

3. Mix in the eggs, one at a time, then mix in the vanilla extract, peppermint extract, and green food coloring until fully combined, making sure to stop and scrape down the sides of the bowl as needed.

4. Mix in the dry ingredients until just combined, then mix in the chocolate chips on low speed until fully incorporated.

5. Cover tightly and refrigerate for at least 2 hours.

6. Preheat the oven to 350°F (180°C). Line large baking sheets with parchment paper or silicone baking mats and set aside.

7. Using a 1½-tablespoon cookie scoop, scoop the cookie dough onto the prepared baking sheets, making sure to leave 1½ to 2 inches (4 to 5 cm) between each one.

8. Bake for 9 to 12 minutes, or until the tops of the cookies are set. Remove from the oven, and allow the cookies to cool on the baking sheets for 5 to 10 minutes, then carefully transfer the cookies to a wire rack to cool completely.

9. Store the cookies in an airtight container at room temperature for up to 1 week.

LUCKY CHARMS COOKIES

YIELD: 36 to 38 cookies

TOTAL TIME: 1 hour 42 minutes
(includes 1 hour of chilling time)

Who doesn't find Lucky Charms "magically delicious"? That's why I decided to use this classic cereal in a homemade cookie dough. The cookies contain not only Lucky Charms marshmallows (the best part, right?) but also crushed-up cereal that is added to the dough.

2½ cups (100 g) Lucky Charms cereal (just the cereal, no marshmallows)

2 cups (250 g) all-purpose flour, spooned and leveled

1 teaspoon baking soda

¾ teaspoon salt

1 cup (2 sticks, or 230 g) unsalted butter, softened

1 cup (200 g) packed light brown sugar

⅓ cup (65 g) granulated sugar

2 large eggs, at room temperature

2 teaspoons pure vanilla extract

¾ cup (140 g) white chocolate chips

1½ cups (55 g) Lucky Charms marshmallows

PRO BAKING TIP

I suggest separating the cereal and marshmallows before getting started with the recipe.

1. Add the cereal to a blender or food processor and process until you have fine crumbs.

2. In a large mixing bowl, whisk together the crushed cereal, flour, baking soda, and salt until well combined. Set aside.

3. In the bowl of a stand mixer fitted with the paddle attachment or in a large mixing bowl using a handheld mixer, beat the butter, brown sugar, and granulated sugar together for 1 to 2 minutes, or until well combined.

4. Mix in the eggs, one at a time, then mix in the vanilla extract until fully combined, making sure to stop and scrape down the sides of the bowl as needed.

5. Mix in the dry ingredients until just combined, then mix in the white chocolate chips on low speed until fully incorporated. Gently fold in the Lucky Charms marshmallows.

6. Cover tightly and refrigerate for at least 1 hour.

7. Preheat the oven to 350°F (180°C). Line large baking sheets with parchment paper or silicone baking mats and set aside.

8. Using a 1½-tablespoon cookie scoop, scoop the cookie dough onto the prepared baking sheets, making sure to leave 1½ to 2 inches (4 to 5 cm) between each one.

9. Bake for 10 to 12 minutes, or until the tops of the cookies are set and the edges are lightly browned. Remove from the oven, and allow the cookies to cool on the baking sheets for 5 to 10 minutes, then carefully transfer the cookies to a wire rack to cool completely.

10. Store the cookies in an airtight container at room temperature for up to 5 days.

BIRD'S NEST COOKIES

YIELD: 26 to 28 cookies

TOTAL TIME: 1 hour
(includes 30 minutes of chilling time)

One of my favorite candies at Easter are chocolate eggs! Between their crunchy outer shell and the creamy chocolate center, they are a delightful treat. Aside from eating them, I love to use them on top of these adorable bird's nest cookies. These no-bake cookies are also incredibly simple to throw together and perfect for making with kids too!

1 bag (12 ounces, or 340 g) semisweet chocolate chips

1 bag (10 ounces, or 283 g) peanut butter chips

5 cups (285 g) chow mein noodles

1 bag (10 ounces, or 283 g) mini chocolate eggs (such as Cadbury Mini Eggs)

PRO BAKING TIP
If you can't find any chocolate eggs, you can use another pastel-colored candy.

1. Line two large baking sheets with parchment paper or silicone baking mats. Set aside.

2. Add the semisweet chocolate chips and peanut butter chips to a large microwave-safe bowl, and stir until well combined.

3. Microwave in 20-second increments, stirring well after each increment, until completely melted and smooth.

4. Add the chow mein noodles. and stir until all the noodles are coated with the chocolate-peanut butter mixture.

5. Scoop large spoonfuls of the mixture, about 2 tablespoons in size, onto the prepared baking sheets. Form into a circle and flatten each one slightly.

6. Top each one with 3 mini chocolate eggs, then transfer the cookies to the refrigerator to chill for 20 to 30 minutes, or until the chocolate is firm and the cookies are set.

7. Store the cookies in an airtight container at room temperature or in the refrigerator for up to 1 week.

FUNFETTI SUGAR COOKIES

YIELD: 32 cookies

TOTAL TIME: 38 minutes

NO CHILLING REQUIRED!

I couldn't pass up a chance to add some sprinkles somewhere in this cookbook, so I figured what better way than in a funfetti sugar cookie. These soft cookies would be perfect for just about any holiday or birthday party; just change out the color of sprinkles!

2¾ cups (345 g) all-purpose flour, spooned and leveled

2 teaspoons cornstarch

1 teaspoon baking powder

½ teaspoon salt

1 cup (2 sticks, or 230 g) unsalted butter, softened

1⅓ cups (270 g) granulated sugar

1 large egg, at room temperature

1 large egg yolk, at room temperature

2 teaspoons pure vanilla extract

⅓ cup (65 g) sprinkles

PRO BAKING TIP

I suggest using longer sprinkles, also known as jimmies, in these cookies. I have found that round sprinkles, also known as nonpareil sprinkles, tend to bleed their color into the cookie dough.

1. Preheat the oven to 350°F (180°C). Line large baking sheets with parchment paper or silicone baking mats and set aside.

2. In a large mixing bowl, whisk together the flour, cornstarch, baking powder, and salt. Set aside.

3. In the bowl of a stand mixer fitted with the paddle attachment or in a large mixing bowl using a handheld mixer, beat the butter and granulated sugar together for 1 to 2 minutes, or until well combined.

4. Mix in the egg, egg yolk, and vanilla extract until fully combined, making sure to stop and scrape down the sides of the bowl as needed.

5. Mix in the dry ingredients until just combined, then gently stir in the sprinkles.

6. Using a 1½-tablespoon cookie scoop, scoop the cookie dough onto the prepared baking sheets, making sure to leave 1½ to 2 inches (4 to 5 cm) between each one. Gently press each ball of cookie dough down to slightly flatten it.

7. Bake for 10 to 13 minutes, or until the tops of the cookies are set. Remove from the oven, and allow the cookies to cool on the baking sheets for 5 to 10 minutes, then transfer the cookies to a wire rack to cool completely.

8. Store the cookies in an airtight container at room temperature for up to 1 week.

CHOCOLATE CHIP COOKIE CAKE

YIELD: one 9-inch (23 cm) cookie cake

TOTAL TIME: 1 hour 8 minutes

NO CHILLING REQUIRED!

Because who wants to have to choose between a cookie or a cake? Now you don't have to! This cake tastes just like a chocolate chip cookie.

CHOCOLATE CHIP COOKIE CAKE

Nonstick cooking spray, for greasing the pan

2 cups (250 g) all-purpose flour, spooned and leveled

½ teaspoon baking soda

¾ teaspoon salt

¾ cup (1½ sticks, or 170 g) unsalted butter, softened

¾ cup (150 g) packed light brown sugar

¼ cup (50 g) granulated sugar

1 large egg, at room temperature

1 large egg yolk, at room temperature

1 teaspoon pure vanilla extract

1 cup (190 g) semisweet chocolate chips

CHOCOLATE BUTTERCREAM FROSTING

½ cup (1 stick, or 115 g) unsalted butter, softened

1½ cups (180 g) powdered sugar

¼ cup (22 g) natural unsweetened cocoa powder

2 tablespoons (30 ml) heavy whipping cream

½ teaspoon pure vanilla extract

Tiny pinch of salt (optional)

1. **To make the chocolate chip cookie cake:** Preheat the oven to 350°F (180°C). Spray a 9-inch (23 cm) springform pan with nonstick cooking spray and set aside.

2. In a large mixing bowl, whisk together the flour, baking soda, and salt. Set aside.

3. In the bowl of a stand mixer fitted with the paddle attachment or in a large mixing bowl using a handheld mixer, beat the butter, brown sugar, and granulated sugar together for 1 to 2 minutes, or until well combined. Mix in the egg, egg yolk, and vanilla extract until fully combined, making sure to stop and scrape down the sides of the bowl as needed.

4. Mix in the dry ingredients until just combined, then mix in the chocolate chips on low speed until fully incorporated.

5. Scoop the cookie dough into the prepared springform pan and spread it out in one even layer. Bake for 22 to 28 minutes, or until the top of the cake is set and lightly browned. Cover loosely with foil if needed to prevent excess browning. Remove from the oven, and allow to cool completely in the pan.

6. **To make the chocolate buttercream frosting:** In the bowl of a stand mixer fitted with the paddle or whisk attachment or in a large mixing bowl using a handheld mixer, beat the butter for 1 to 2 minutes, or until smooth. Add the powdered sugar, ½ cup (60 g) at a time, mixing in each addition until well combined.

7. Add the cocoa powder and mix until fully combined, then add the heavy whipping cream, vanilla extract, and salt (if using), and continue mixing until well combined, stopping to scrape down the sides of the bowl as needed.

8. Release the cooled cookie cake from the springform pan. Add the frosting to a piping bag with a piping tip (I used Wilton 1M), and pipe around the edges of the cookie cake.

9. Store the cookie cake in an airtight container at room temperature or in the refrigerator for up to 4 days.

PRO BAKING TIP

If you prefer a regular vanilla frosting, leave out the cocoa powder and only use 1 tablespoon (15 ml) of heavy whipping cream.

FOURTH OF JULY COOKIE CUPS

YIELD: 24 cookie cups

TOTAL TIME: 53 minutes

NO CHILLING REQUIRED!

These Fourth of July–inspired cookie cups are made with a sugar cookie base and filled with a vanilla buttercream frosting that takes them over the top. Just don't leave off the festive sprinkles!

SUGAR COOKIE CUPS

Nonstick cooking spray, for greasing the pan

1½ cups (190 g) all-purpose flour, spooned and leveled

1 teaspoon cornstarch

½ teaspoon baking powder

¼ teaspoon salt

½ cup (1 stick, or 115 g) unsalted butter, softened

¾ cup (150 g) granulated sugar

1 large egg, at room temperature

1 teaspoon pure vanilla extract

Red, white, and blue sprinkles, for topping

VANILLA BUTTERCREAM FROSTING

½ cup (1 stick, or 115 g) unsalted butter, softened

1½ cups (180 g) powdered sugar

1 tablespoon (15 ml) heavy whipping cream

1 teaspoon pure vanilla extract

PRO BAKING TIP

You can use different colors of sprinkles and make these cookie cups for any holiday!

1. **To make the sugar cookie cups:** Preheat the oven to 350°F (180°C). Spray a 24-count mini muffin pan with nonstick cooking spray and set aside.

2. In a large mixing bowl, whisk together the flour, cornstarch, baking powder, and salt. Set aside.

3. In the bowl of a stand mixer fitted with the paddle attachment or in a large mixing bowl using a handheld mixer, beat the butter and granulated sugar together for 1 to 2 minutes, or until well combined.

4. Mix in the egg and vanilla extract until fully combined, making sure to stop and scrape down the sides of the bowl as needed.

5. Mix in the dry ingredients until just combined.

6. Evenly distribute the cookie dough among all 24 cups in the mini muffin pan, a little more than 1 tablespoon of cookie dough per cup. Press each ball of cookie dough into the cups and smooth it out.

7. Bake for 11 to 13 minutes, or until the edges of the cookie cups are lightly browned and the tops are set.

8. Remove from the oven, and make an indention in each cookie using the back of a measuring teaspoon. Allow to cool completely in the muffin pan, then carefully remove from the pan and set aside.

9. **To make the vanilla buttercream frosting:** In the bowl of a stand mixer fitted with the paddle or whisk attachment or in a large mixing bowl using a handheld mixer, beat the butter for 1 to 2 minutes, or until smooth. Add the powdered sugar, ½ cup (60 g) at a time, mixing in each addition until well combined.

10. Add the heavy whipping cream and vanilla extract, and continue mixing until fully combined, stopping to scrape down the sides of the bowl as needed.

11. Add the frosting to a piping bag with a piping tip (I used Wilton 1M), and pipe on top of the cooled cookie cups. Top with sprinkles.

12. Store the cookie cups in an airtight container at room temperature or in the refrigerator for up to 4 days.

PUMPKIN COOKIES

YIELD: 18 to 20 cookies

TOTAL TIME: 38 minutes

NO CHILLING REQUIRED!

As soon as the air starts to cool off and the leaves start to turn, I love to break out the cans of pumpkin puree and start baking with them! One of my favorite ways to use it is in these pumpkin cookies. Unlike other pumpkin cookies, these cookies are soft but not cakey.

1½ cups (190 g) all-purpose flour, spooned and leveled

1 teaspoon pumpkin pie spice

½ teaspoon ground cinnamon

½ teaspoon baking soda

¼ teaspoon salt

½ cup (1 stick, or 115 g) unsalted butter, softened

½ cup (100 g) granulated sugar

¼ cup (50 g) packed light brown sugar

¼ cup (60 g) pumpkin puree

1 large egg yolk, at room temperature (see Pro Baking Tip)

1 teaspoon pure vanilla extract

> ## PRO BAKING TIP
> You may notice that this recipe calls only for an egg yolk instead of a whole egg, but I promise this isn't a mistake! I've found that the pumpkin adds moisture and almost acts as an egg in this recipe, so you only need the yolk.

1. Preheat the oven to 350°F (180°C). Line two large baking sheets with parchment paper or silicone baking mats and set aside.

2. In a large mixing bowl, whisk together the flour, pumpkin pie spice, ground cinnamon, baking soda, and salt until well combined. Set aside.

3. In the bowl of a stand mixer fitted with the paddle attachment or in a large mixing bowl using a handheld mixer, beat the butter, granulated sugar, and brown sugar together for 1 to 2 minutes, or until well combined.

4. Mix in the pumpkin puree, egg yolk, and vanilla extract until fully combined, making sure to stop and scrape down the sides of the bowl as needed.

5. Mix in the dry ingredients until just combined.

6. Using a 1½-tablespoon cookie scoop, scoop the cookie dough onto the prepared baking sheets, making sure to leave 1½ to 2 inches (4 to 5 cm) between each one.

7. Bake for 11 to 13 minutes, or until the tops of the cookie are set. Remove from the oven, and allow the cookies to cool on the baking sheets for 5 to 10 minutes, then carefully transfer the cookies to a wire rack to cool completely.

8. Store the cookies in an airtight container at room temperature for up to 5 days.

PUMPKIN WHOOPIE PIES

YIELD: 16 whoopie pies

TOTAL TIME: 54 minutes

NO CHILLING REQUIRED!

If you love pumpkin bread, you are going to love these whoopie pies! The cookie base is soft, moist, cakey, and packed with pumpkin flavor, and the cream cheese frosting takes these delicious whoopie pies to the next level.

PUMPKIN COOKIES

2 cups (250 g) all-purpose flour, spooned and leveled

1 teaspoon baking soda

1 teaspoon baking powder

2 teaspoons pumpkin pie spice

½ teaspoon ground cinnamon

½ teaspoon salt

½ cup (1 stick, or 115 g) unsalted butter, softened

1 cup (200 g) packed light brown sugar

2 large eggs, at room temperature

1 cup (250 g) pumpkin puree

1½ teaspoons pure vanilla extract

CREAM CHEESE FROSTING

6 ounces (170 g) brick-style cream cheese, softened

6 tablespoons (85 g) unsalted butter, softened

1½ cups (180 g) powdered sugar

½ teaspoon pure vanilla extract

PRO BAKING TIP

Make sure to use pumpkin puree and not pumpkin pie filling in these cookies. Pumpkin pie filling is already sweetened and has spices added to it.

1. **To make the pumpkin cookies:** Preheat the oven to 350°F (180°C). Line large baking sheets with parchment paper or silicone baking mats and set aside.

2. In a large mixing bowl, whisk together the flour, baking soda, baking powder, pumpkin pie spice, ground cinnamon, and salt until well combined. Set aside.

3. In the bowl of a stand mixer fitted with the paddle attachment or in a large mixing bowl using a handheld mixer, beat the butter and brown sugar together for 1 to 2 minutes, or until well combined.

4. Mix in the eggs, one at a time, then mix in the pumpkin puree and vanilla extract until fully combined, making sure to stop and scrape down the sides of the bowl as needed.

5. Mix in the dry ingredients until just combined.

6. Using a 1½-tablespoon cookie scoop, scoop the cookie dough onto the prepared baking sheets, making sure to leave 1½ to 2 inches (4 to 5 cm) between each one.

7. Bake for 12 to 14 minutes, or until the tops of the cookies are set and spring back when touched lightly. Remove from the oven, and allow the cookies to cool on the baking sheets for 5 to 10 minutes, then carefully transfer the cookies to a wire rack to cool completely.

8. **To make the cream cheese frosting:** In the bowl of a stand mixer fitted with the paddle attachment, or in a large mixing bowl using a handheld mixer, beat the cream cheese until smooth.

9. Add the butter and mix for about 30 seconds to 1 minute, or until well combined and smooth. Add the powdered sugar and vanilla extract and continue mixing until fully combined, stopping to scrape down the sides of the bowl as needed.

10. Once the cookies have cooled completely, pipe the frosting on the flat side of half of the cookies, then top with the other half of the cookies.

11. Store the cookies in an airtight container in the refrigerator for up to 4 days.

APPLE CINNAMON SNICKERDOODLES

YIELD: 60 to 62 cookies

TOTAL TIME: 1 hour 52 minutes
(includes 1 hour of chilling time)

This simple cookie recipe is a fun twist on the classic snickerdoodle, with extra cinnamon, brown sugar, and chopped apples. It's like the taste of fall wrapped up in a delicious cookie.

APPLE SNICKERDOODLE COOKIES

3 cups (375 g) all-purpose flour, spooned and leveled

2 teaspoons cream of tartar

1 teaspoon baking soda

1½ teaspoons ground cinnamon

½ teaspoon salt

1 cup (2 sticks, or 230 g) unsalted butter, softened

¾ cup (150 g) granulated sugar

¾ cup (150 g) packed light brown sugar

1 large egg, at room temperature

1 large egg yolk, at room temperature

2 teaspoons pure vanilla extract

1¼ cups (155 g) chopped peeled apple

CINNAMON SUGAR COATING

¼ cup (50 g) granulated sugar

2 teaspoons ground cinnamon

1. **To make the apple snickerdoodle cookies:** In a large mixing bowl, whisk together the flour, cream of tartar, baking soda, 1½ teaspoons ground cinnamon, and salt. Set aside.

2. In the bowl of a stand mixer fitted with the paddle attachment or in a large mixing bowl using a handheld mixer, beat the butter, ¾ cup (150 g) granulated sugar, and brown sugar together for 1 to 2 minutes, or until well combined.

3. Mix in the egg, egg yolk, and vanilla extract until fully combined, making sure to stop and scrape down the sides of the bowl as needed.

4. Mix in the dry ingredients until just combined, then gently fold in the chopped apples.

5. Cover tightly and refrigerate for at least 1 hour.

6. Preheat the oven to 375°F (190°C). Line large baking sheets with parchment paper or silicone baking mats and set aside.

7. **To make the cinnamon sugar coating:** In a small mixing bowl, whisk together the ¼ cup (50 g) granulated sugar and 2 teaspoons ground cinnamon. Using a 1-tablespoon cookie scoop, scoop the cookie dough, roll it into a ball, and coat it in the cinnamon sugar mixture. Place each ball of cookie dough onto the prepared baking sheets, making sure to leave 1½ to 2 inches (4 to 5 cm) between each one.

8. Bake for 9 to 12 minutes, or until the tops of the cookies are set. Remove from the oven, and allow the cookies to cool on the baking sheets for 5 to 10 minutes, then carefully transfer the cookies to a wire rack to cool completely.

9. Store the cookies in an airtight container at room temperature for up to 3 days.

PRO BAKING TIP

You can use any kind of baking apple for this recipe; some of my favorites are Granny Smith or Honeycrisp apples. Be sure to peel, core, and finely dice your apples.

CHRISTMAS COOKIES

One of my favorite times of year to bake cookies is Christmas.
So naturally, I knew that I needed to conclude this cookbook with
a chapter dedicated to the ultimate cookie-baking season!

In the next few pages, you will find a mix of classic
Christmas cookies, such as cutout sugar cookies, spritz cookies,
and pinwheels. But I didn't want to just share the classics; there
are also some fun treats in this chapter that are perfect for the
winter holiday.

I've even included a bonus recipe for you—my easy sugar
cookie icing!

CUTOUT SUGAR COOKIES

YIELD: 25 to 30 cookies

TOTAL TIME: 3 hours 43 minutes
    (includes 2 hours of chilling time)

Sometimes it can be hard to find a cutout sugar cookie recipe that tastes delicious and holds its shape. This simple cookie recipe checks both of those boxes!

2¾ cups (345 g) all-purpose flour, spooned and leveled

¾ teaspoon baking powder

½ teaspoon salt

1 cup (2 sticks, or 230 g) unsalted butter, softened

1 cup (200 g) granulated sugar

1 large egg, at room temperature

2 teaspoons pure vanilla extract

1 batch Easy Sugar Cookie Icing (page 166)

Sprinkles, sanding sugar, and dragees, for topping (optional)

PRO BAKING TIP

To roll out the dough to an even thickness, I recommend placing a ¼-inch-thick (6 mm) square dowel on each side of the dough, then rolling it out with a rolling pin going over the dowels.

1. In a large mixing bowl, whisk together the flour, baking powder, and salt until well combined. Set aside.

2. In the bowl of a stand mixer fitted with the paddle attachment or in a large mixing bowl using a handheld mixer, beat the butter and granulated sugar together for 1 to 2 minutes, or until well combined.

3. Mix in the egg and vanilla extract until fully combined, making sure to stop and scrape down the sides of the bowl as needed.

4. Mix in the dry ingredients until just combined.

5. Divide the dough in half. Lightly flour a piece of parchment paper, add half of the dough, flour the top of the dough, and then top with another piece of parchment paper. Roll out the dough between the pieces of parchment paper to ¼ inch (6 mm) thick with a rolling pin. Repeat with the other half of the dough between two additional pieces of parchment paper.

6. Leaving the sheets of dough between the parchment paper, place on a baking sheet and refrigerate for at least 2 hours.

7. Preheat the oven to 350°F (180°C). Line large baking sheets with parchment paper or silicone baking mats and set aside.

8. Remove one sheet of dough from the refrigerator and peel off the top layer of parchment paper. Using 2½- to 3-inch (6 to 7.5 cm) cookie cutters, cut the cookie dough into shapes, and place them onto the prepared baking sheets, making sure to leave 1½ to 2 inches (4 to 5 cm) between each one.

9. Roll any scrap pieces of dough between the parchment paper, and continue cutting out shapes. Repeat with the other sheet of chilled cookie dough.

10. Bake for 11 to 13 minutes, or until the tops of the cookies are set. Remove from the oven, and allow the cookies to cool on the baking sheets for 10 minutes, then carefully transfer the cookies to a wire rack to cool completely.

11. Decorate the cooled sugar cookies with the icing and sprinkles (if using). Place the cookies in a single layer in airtight containers, and allow the icing to harden fully for 20 to 24 hours. Then stack and store the cookies in an airtight container at room temperature for up to 1 week.

EASY SUGAR COOKIE ICING

YIELD: 1¾ cups (575 g)

TOTAL TIME: 15 minutes

If you are looking for a simple icing that you can use to beautifully decorate cookies, then look no further! This recipe includes instructions for both the outline and fill icings, and uses just a few simple ingredients, tastes delicious, and dries hard, so you can stack your cookies.

4 cups (480 g) powdered sugar, plus more if needed

6 tablespoons (90 ml) milk, divided, plus more if needed

4 teaspoons light corn syrup

1 teaspoon pure vanilla extract

Gel food coloring (optional)

PRO BAKING TIP

I recommend using gel food coloring in this icing, since liquid food coloring can thin it out.

1. **To make the outline icing:** In a large mixing bowl, whisk together the powdered sugar, 5 tablespoons (75 ml) of the milk, light corn syrup, and vanilla extract until well combined and no lumps remain. The mixture will be pretty thick.

2. Mix in 1 teaspoon of milk at a time until the icing has thinned out and reached an outline consistency. To test the icing, lift the whisk or spoon from the mixing bowl; you should see ribbons of icing falling back into the bowl for 3 to 4 seconds. If needed, add more milk to thin out the icing or more powdered sugar to make it thicker.

3. Mix in the gel food coloring (if using) until fully combined. Remove one-third of the mixture for the outline icing and set aside.

4. **To make the fill icing:** Add ½ to 1 teaspoon of milk at a time to the remaining two-thirds of the mixture until the icing reaches a filling consistency. When you lift your whisk or spoon from the bowl, the icing should quickly melt back into the bowl of icing.

5. To decorate your cookies, place the outline icing and fill icing in separate piping bags, and cut a small piece of the tip off each one. Outline each cookie with the outline icing, then use the fill icing to fill in the cookie. Use a toothpick if needed to move the icing around and fill in any empty spots.

6. Place the cookies in a single layer in airtight containers, and allow the icing to harden fully for 20 to 24 hours before stacking the cookies.

HOT COCOA COOKIES

YIELD: 18 to 20 cookies

TOTAL TIME: 1 hour 38 minutes
(includes 45 minutes of chilling time)

During the cold winter months, there is nothing better than curling up under a warm blanket with a cup of hot cocoa. These cookies use a homemade chocolate cookie base, and they are then topped off with marshmallows and even more chocolate. Just like a cup of hot cocoa in the form of a soft, gooey cookie!

1¼ cups (160 g) all-purpose flour, spooned and leveled

⅓ cup (30 g) natural unsweetened cocoa powder

½ teaspoon baking soda

¼ teaspoon salt

½ cup (1 stick, or 115 g) unsalted butter, softened

½ cup (100 g) packed light brown sugar

½ cup (100 g) granulated sugar

1 large egg, at room temperature

1 teaspoon pure vanilla extract

9 or 10 regular marshmallows, cut in half

4 ounces (113 g) semisweet chocolate, roughly chopped

PRO BAKING TIP

If you want the melted chocolate to set faster, place the cookies in the refrigerator for 10 to 15 minutes.

1. In a large mixing bowl, sift the flour and cocoa powder together, then whisk in the baking soda and salt until well combined. Set aside.

2. In the bowl of a stand mixer fitted with the paddle attachment or in a large mixing bowl using a handheld mixer, beat the butter, brown sugar, and granulated sugar together for 1 to 2 minutes, or until well combined.

3. Mix in the egg and vanilla extract until fully combined, making sure to stop and scrape down the sides of the bowl as needed.

4. Mix in the dry ingredients until just combined.

5. Cover tightly and refrigerate for at least 45 minutes.

6. Preheat the oven to 350°F (180°C). Line two large baking sheets with parchment paper or silicone baking mats and set aside.

7. Using a 1½-tablespoon cookie scoop, scoop the cookie dough, roll it into a ball, and place it onto the prepared baking sheets, making sure to leave 1½ to 2 inches (4 to 5 cm) between each one.

8. Bake for 9 to 10 minutes, or until the tops of the cookies are just set. Remove from the oven, and gently press half of a marshmallow into the top of each cookie. Return to the oven and bake for an additional 2 to 3 minutes, or until the marshmallows are softened. Remove from the oven, and allow the cookies to cool on the baking sheets for 5 to 10 minutes, then carefully transfer the cookies to a wire rack to cool completely.

9. Add the chopped chocolate to a microwave-safe bowl. Microwave in 20- to 30-second increments, making sure to stir well after each increment, until completely melted and smooth. Drizzle the melted chocolate on top of each cookie.

10. Store the cookies in an airtight container at room temperature for up to 5 days.

SPRITZ COOKIES

YIELD: 84 to 96 cookies

TOTAL TIME: 43 minutes

NO CHILLING REQUIRED!

I couldn't resist adding this adorable
classic Christmas cookie in this chapter!
The dough is incredibly easy to throw
together, can be colored however you
prefer, and can also be made in a variety
of different shapes.

1 cup (2 sticks, or 230 g) unsalted butter,
  softened

⅔ cup (135 g) granulated sugar

1 large egg, at room temperature

1½ teaspoons pure vanilla extract

2½ cups (315 g) all-purpose flour, spooned
  and leveled

¼ teaspoon salt

Food coloring (optional)

Sprinkles and sanding sugar, for topping
  (optional)

1. Preheat the oven to 400°F (204°C). Place three large baking sheets in the refrigerator.

2. In the bowl of a stand mixer fitted with the paddle attachment or in a large mixing bowl using a handheld mixer, beat the butter and granulated sugar together for 1 to 2 minutes, or until well combined.

3. Mix in the egg and vanilla extract until fully combined, making sure to stop and scrape down the sides of the bowl as needed.

4. Mix in the flour and salt until just combined. Equally divide the cookie dough into the amount of different colors for the cookies, and mix in the food coloring (if using) until fully combined.

5. Press the dough into a cookie press fitted with a template. Remove the baking sheets from the refrigerator, and press the dough onto the chilled ungreased baking sheets. Top each cookie with sprinkles (if using).

6. Bake for 6 to 8 minutes, or until the tops of the cookies are just set. Remove from the oven, and carefully slide a thin spatula under all the cookies to prevent them from sticking to the baking sheets.

7. Allow the cookies to cool completely, then remove them from the baking sheets.

8. Store the cookies in an airtight container at room temperature for up to 1 week.

PRO BAKING TIPS

✶ Chill your baking sheets in the refrigerator while you make the cookie dough. This step will help the cookies hold their shape while baking.

✶ Be sure to run a thin spatula under the cookies as soon as they come out of the oven. This will help prevent them from getting stuck to the pan as they cool.

CANDY CANE SUGAR COOKIES

YIELD: 32 cookies

TOTAL TIME: 1 hour 28 minutes
    (includes 20 minutes of chilling time)

Do you ever end up with some extra candy canes around Christmas? If so, this recipe is a wonderful way to use them! The base of these cookies uses my easy sugar cookie dough, and then the baked cookies are dipped in white chocolate and topped with crushed candy canes.

2¾ cups (345 g) all-purpose flour, spooned and leveled

2 teaspoons cornstarch

1 teaspoon baking powder

½ teaspoon salt

1 cup (2 sticks, or 230 g) unsalted butter, softened

1⅓ cups (270 g) granulated sugar

1 large egg, at room temperature

1 large egg yolk, at room temperature

1 teaspoon pure vanilla extract

1 teaspoon peppermint extract

12 ounces (340 g) white chocolate, roughly chopped

10 regular-size candy canes (140 g), crushed

PRO BAKING TIP
Feel free to swap out the white chocolate in this recipe with semisweet, dark, or even milk chocolate.

1. Preheat the oven to 350°F (180°C). Line large baking sheets with parchment paper or silicone baking mats and set aside.

2. In a large mixing bowl, whisk together the flour, cornstarch, baking powder, and salt. Set aside.

3. In the bowl of a stand mixer fitted with the paddle attachment or in a large mixing bowl using a handheld mixer, beat the butter and granulated sugar together for 1 to 2 minutes, or until well combined.

4. Mix in the egg, egg yolk, vanilla extract, and peppermint extract until fully combined, making sure to stop and scrape down the sides of the bowl as needed.

5. Mix in the dry ingredients until just combined.

6. Using a 1½-tablespoon cookie scoop, scoop the cookie dough onto the prepared baking sheets, making sure to leave 1½ to 2 inches (4 to 5 cm) between each one. Gently press each ball of cookie dough down to slightly flatten it.

7. Bake for 10 to 13 minutes, or until the tops of the cookies are set. Remove from the oven, and allow the cookies to cool on the baking sheets for 5 to 10 minutes, then carefully transfer the cookies to a wire rack to cool completely.

8. Line a separate baking sheet with parchment paper or a silicone baking mat. Set aside.

9. Add the chopped white chocolate to a microwave-safe bowl. Microwave in 20- to 30-second increments, stirring well after each increment, until completely melted and smooth.

10. Dip half of a cookie in the melted white chocolate, place on the prepared baking sheet, and sprinkle with the crushed candy canes. Repeat with the remaining cookies.

11. Transfer the cookies to the refrigerator to chill for 15 to 20 minutes, or until the chocolate has hardened.

12. Store the cookies in an airtight container at room temperature for up to 1 week.

SOUR CREAM COOKIES

YIELD: 22 cookies

TOTAL TIME: 1 hour

NO CHILLING REQUIRED!

If you are a fan of cakey cookies, then these simple sour cream sugar cookies are for you! They are incredibly moist and soft thanks to the sour cream, and they are topped off with an easy vanilla buttercream frosting.

SOUR CREAM COOKIES

1½ cups (190 g) all-purpose flour, spooned and leveled

1 teaspoon baking powder

¼ teaspoon salt

½ cup (1 stick, or 115 g) unsalted butter, softened

¾ cup (150 g) granulated sugar

1 large egg, at room temperature

1½ teaspoons pure vanilla extract

½ cup (120 g) sour cream, at room temperature

VANILLA BUTTERCREAM FROSTING

½ cup (1 stick, or 115 g) unsalted butter, softened

1½ cups (180 g) powdered sugar

1 tablespoon (15 ml) heavy whipping cream

1 teaspoon pure vanilla extract

Gel food coloring (optional)

PRO BAKING TIP

If you prefer a chocolate frosting, try the frosting recipe from the Chocolate Chip Cookie Cake (page 153).

1. **To make the sour cream cookies:** Preheat the oven to 350°F (180°C). Line two large baking sheets with parchment paper or silicone baking mats and set aside.

2. In a large mixing bowl, whisk together the flour, baking powder, and salt until well combined. Set aside.

3. In the bowl of a stand mixer fitted with the paddle attachment or in a large mixing bowl using a handheld mixer, beat the butter and granulated sugar together for 1 to 2 minutes, or until well combined.

4. Mix in the egg and vanilla extract until fully combined, making sure to stop and scrape down the sides of the bowl as needed.

5. Mix in the dry ingredients in 2 additions, alternating with the sour cream. Make sure to mix in each addition until just combined, and be careful not to overmix the batter.

6. Using a 1½-tablespoon cookie scoop, scoop the cookie dough onto the prepared baking sheets, making sure to leave 1½ to 2 inches (4 to 5 cm) between each one.

7. Bake for 14 to 16 minutes, or until the tops of the cookies are set and spring back when touched lightly. Remove from the oven, and allow the cookies to cool on the baking sheets for 10 minutes, then carefully transfer the cookies to a wire rack to cool completely.

8. **To make the vanilla buttercream frosting:** In the bowl of a stand mixer fitted with the paddle or whisk attachment or in a large mixing bowl using a handheld mixer, beat the butter for 1 to 2 minutes, or until smooth. Add the powdered sugar, ½ cup (60 g) at a time, mixing in each addition until well combined.

9. Add the heavy whipping cream, vanilla extract, and gel food coloring (if using), and continue mixing until fully combined.

10. Once the cookies have cooled completely, spread the frosting on top of the cookies.

11. Store the cookies in an airtight container at room temperature or in the refrigerator for up to 4 days.

CINNAMON ROLL SUGAR COOKIES

YIELD: 48 cookies

TOTAL TIME: 3 hours 18 minutes
(includes 2 hours of chilling time)

Imagine a soft sugar cookie that tastes like a cinnamon roll. The result? These cinnamon roll sugar cookies! Don't omit the icing; it's the perfect final touch.

SUGAR COOKIE DOUGH

2¾ cups (345 g) all-purpose flour, spooned and leveled

½ teaspoon baking powder

½ teaspoon ground cinnamon

½ teaspoon salt

1 cup (2 sticks, or 230 g) unsalted butter, softened

1 cup (200 g) granulated sugar

1 large egg, at room temperature

2 teaspoons pure vanilla extract

CINNAMON SUGAR FILLING

2 tablespoons (30 g) unsalted butter, melted and slightly cooled

⅓ cup (65 g) packed light brown sugar

2 teaspoons ground cinnamon

VANILLA ICING

1½ cups (180 g) powdered sugar

3 tablespoons (45 ml) whole milk, divided

½ teaspoon pure vanilla extract

1. **To make the sugar cookie dough:** In a large mixing bowl, whisk together the flour, baking powder, ground cinnamon, and salt until well combined. Set aside.

2. In the bowl of a stand mixer fitted with the paddle attachment or in a large mixing bowl using a handheld mixer, beat the butter and granulated sugar together for 1 to 2 minutes, or until well combined.

3. Mix in the egg and vanilla extract until fully combined, making sure to stop and scrape down the sides of the bowl as needed.

4. Mix in the dry ingredients until just combined.

5. Divide the dough in half. Lightly flour a piece of parchment paper, add half of the dough, flour the top of the dough, and then top with another piece of parchment paper. Roll out the dough between the parchment paper into an 8 x 10-inch (20 x 25 cm) rectangle with a rolling pin. Repeat with the other half of the dough between two additional pieces of parchment paper.

6. **To make the cinnamon sugar filling:** Peel off the top layer of parchment paper from each sheet of dough. Brush the top of the dough with the melted butter. Combine the brown sugar and ground cinnamon in a small bowl. Sprinkle the mixture on top of both sheets of dough, making sure to cover them completely.

7. Starting at the longer end, roll each piece of dough into a 10-inch-long (25 cm) log. Wrap each log tightly with plastic wrap, and chill in the refrigerator for at least 2 hours.

8. Preheat the oven to 350°F (180°C). Line large baking sheets with parchment paper or silicone baking mats and set aside.

9. Remove the cookie dough from the refrigerator, and peel off the plastic wrap. Cut the ends off each log, and then slice it into ⅜-inch-thick (1 cm) slices, or 24 equal-size slices per log (see the image on page 178 for reference). Place the slices on the prepared baking sheets, making sure to leave 1½ to 2 inches (4 to 5 cm) between each one.

continued

PRO BAKING TIP

As you are rolling the cookie dough in step 7, use the parchment paper under it to help form a tight log, pulling the parchment paper back and then lifting it again as you roll it.

10. Bake for 11 to 13 minutes, or until the tops of the cookies are set and the edges are lightly browned. Remove from the oven, and allow the cookies to cool on the baking sheets for 5 to 10 minutes, then carefully transfer the cookies to a wire rack to cool completely.

11. **To make the vanilla icing:** Whisk together the powdered sugar, 2 tablespoons (30 ml) of the milk, and vanilla extract in a large mixing bowl until well combined and no lumps remain.

12. Mix in ½ teaspoon of the remaining milk at a time until the icing reaches your desired consistency.

13. Drizzle the icing on top of all the cooled cookies.

14. Store the cookies in an airtight container at room temperature for up to 1 week.

PINWHEELS

YIELD: 32 to 34 cookies

TOTAL TIME: 3 hours 4 minutes
(includes 2 hours of chilling time)

I couldn't resist adding one more slice-and-bake recipe to this cookbook. These classic pinwheels have a layer of vanilla dough and chocolate dough that's rolled up into one rich and delicious cookie!

2 ounces (57 g) semisweet chocolate, roughly chopped

2¾ cups (345 g) all-purpose flour, spooned and leveled

½ teaspoon baking powder

½ teaspoon salt

1 cup (2 sticks, or 230 g) unsalted butter, softened

1 cup (200 g) granulated sugar

1 large egg, at room temperature

1½ teaspoons pure vanilla extract

1. Add the chopped semisweet chocolate to a microwave-safe bowl. Microwave in 20- to 30-second increments, stirring well after each increment, until completely melted and smooth. Set aside to cool slightly while you prepare the cookie dough.

2. In a large mixing bowl, whisk together the flour, baking powder, and salt until well combined. Set aside.

3. In the bowl of a stand mixer fitted with the paddle attachment or in a large mixing bowl using a handheld mixer, beat the butter and granulated sugar together for 1 to 2 minutes, or until well combined.

4. Mix in the egg and vanilla extract until fully combined, making sure to stop and scrape down the sides of the bowl as needed.

5. Mix in the dry ingredients until just combined.

6. Divide the dough in half. Add the cooled melted chocolate to one half of the cookie dough, and mix until fully combined.

7. Lightly flour a piece of parchment paper, add the vanilla dough, flour the top of the dough, and then top with another piece of parchment paper. Roll out the dough between the parchment paper into an 9 x 13-inch (23 x 33 cm) rectangle with a rolling pin. Repeat with the chocolate dough between two additional pieces of parchment paper.

8. Peel off the top layer of parchment paper from each sheet of dough. Carefully place the chocolate dough on top of the vanilla dough and peel off the remaining layer of parchment paper. Use a sharp knife or pizza cutter to trim any excess dough from the edges.

9. Starting at the longer end, roll the dough tightly into a 13-inch-long (33 cm) log. Cut the dough in half so you have two 6½- to 7-inch-long (16.5 to 18 cm) logs. Wrap each log tightly with plastic wrap, and chill in the refrigerator for at least 2 hours.

continued

10. Preheat the oven to 350°F (180°C). Line large baking sheets with parchment paper or silicone baking mats and set aside.

11. Remove the cookie dough from the refrigerator and peel off the plastic wrap. Cut the ends off each log, and then slice it into ⅜-inch-thick (1 cm) slices, or 16 or 17 equal-size slices per log. Place the slices on the prepared baking sheets, making sure to leave 1½ to 2 inches (4 to 5 cm) between each one.

12. Bake for 12 to 14 minutes, or until the tops of the cookies are set and the edges are lightly browned. Remove from the oven, and allow the cookies to cool on the baking sheets for 5 to 10 minutes, then carefully transfer the cookies to a wire rack to cool completely.

13. Store the cookies in an airtight container at room temperature for up to 1 week.

CRANBERRY PISTACHIO SLICE-AND-BAKE COOKIES

YIELD: 26 to 28 cookies

TOTAL TIME: 3 hours 55 minutes
(includes 3 hours of chilling time)

Slice-and-bake cookies are some of my favorite cookies to make because they are so simple! This recipe uses a basic shortbread cookie dough, which is filled with chopped pistachios and sweetened dried cranberries. While these cookies are simple, they are also incredibly delicious.

1 cup (2 sticks, or 230 g) unsalted butter, softened

⅔ cup (135 g) granulated sugar

1 large egg yolk, at room temperature

1 teaspoon pure vanilla extract

2⅓ cups (290 g) all-purpose flour, spooned and leveled

¼ teaspoon salt

1 cup (135 g) chopped pistachios

¾ cup (105 g) sweetened dried cranberries

PRO BAKING TIP

I prefer to use roasted and lightly salted pistachios in these cookies, but plain pistachios work just fine.

1. In the bowl of a stand mixer fitted with the paddle attachment or in a large mixing bowl using a handheld mixer, beat the butter and granulated sugar together for 1 to 2 minutes, or until well combined.

2. Mix in the egg yolk and vanilla extract until fully combined, making sure to stop and scrape down the sides of the bowl as needed.

3. Mix in the flour and salt until just combined, then mix in the chopped pistachios and dried cranberries on low speed until fully incorporated.

4. Divide the dough in half, and form two 6-inch-long (15 cm) logs that are 2 inches (5 cm) in diameter. Wrap each log tightly with plastic wrap, and chill in the refrigerator for at least 3 hours.

5. Preheat the oven to 350°F (180°C). Line large baking sheets with parchment paper or silicone baking mats and set aside.

6. Remove the cookie dough from the refrigerator and peel off the plastic wrap. Cut the ends off each log, and then slice it into ⅜-inch-thick (1 cm) slices, or 13 or 14 equal-size slices per log. Place the slices on the prepared baking sheets, making sure to leave 1½ to 2 inches (4 to 5 cm) between each one.

7. Bake for 13 to 15 minutes, or until the tops of the cookies are set and the edges are lightly browned. Remove from the oven, and allow the cookies to cool on the baking sheets for 5 to 10 minutes, then carefully transfer the cookies to a wire rack to cool completely.

8. Store the cookies in an airtight container at room temperature for up to 1 week.

FROSTED SUGAR COOKIE BARS

YIELD: 24 bars

TOTAL TIME: 2 hours 55 minutes
(includes 2 hours of cooling time)

Sugar cookies are one of my favorite treats to make during the holidays. Since they can take quite some time to cut out and frost, I decided to create an easier version of this classic recipe. These bars come together quickly, and they are perfect for just about any holiday too!

SUGAR COOKIE BARS

2½ cups (315 g) all-purpose flour, spooned and leveled

1 teaspoon baking powder

½ teaspoon salt

1 cup (2 sticks, or 230 g) unsalted butter, softened

1¼ cups (250 g) granulated sugar

1 large egg, at room temperature

1 large egg yolk, at room temperature

2 teaspoons pure vanilla extract

VANILLA BUTTERCREAM FROSTING

¾ cup (1½ sticks, or 170 g) unsalted butter, softened

2¼ cups (270 g) powdered sugar

2 tablespoons (30 ml) heavy whipping cream

1½ teaspoons pure vanilla extract

1. **To make the sugar cookie bars:** Preheat the oven to 350°F (180°C). Line a 9 x 13-inch (23 x 33 cm) baking pan with parchment paper or aluminum foil, leaving some overhang for easy removal. Set aside.

2. In a large mixing bowl, whisk together the flour, baking powder, and salt until well combined. Set aside.

3. In the bowl of a stand mixer fitted with the paddle attachment or in a large mixing bowl using a handheld mixer, beat the butter and granulated sugar together for 1 to 2 minutes, or until well combined. Mix in the egg, egg yolk, and vanilla extract until fully combined, making sure to stop and scrape down the sides of the bowl as needed.

4. Mix in the dry ingredients until just combined.

5. Scoop the cookie dough into the prepared baking pan and press it down into one even layer. Bake for 23 to 28 minutes, or until the top is set and the edges are lightly browned. Remove from the oven, and cool completely in the pan on a wire rack.

6. **To make the vanilla buttercream frosting:** In the bowl of a stand mixer fitted with the paddle or whisk attachment or in a large mixing bowl using a handheld mixer, beat the butter for 1 to 2 minutes, or until smooth. Add the powdered sugar, ½ cup (60 g) at a time, mixing in each addition until well combined, then mix in the last ¼ cup (30 g) of powdered sugar until fully combined.

7. Add the heavy whipping cream and vanilla extract and continue mixing until well combined.

8. Frost the cooled sugar cookie bars, lift the bars out of the pan, and slice into pieces.

9. Store the bars in an airtight container in the refrigerator for up to 4 days.

PRO BAKING TIP

Want to add sprinkles? Mix ¼ cup (52 g) of your favorite sprinkles into the cookie dough after you mix in the dry ingredients in step 4. If you want to add a pop of color to your frosting, add 2 to 3 drops of liquid food coloring or a little gel food coloring when you add the whipping cream and vanilla extract in step 7.

GINGERDOODLES

YIELD: 44 to 46 cookies

TOTAL TIME: 1 hour 42 minutes
(includes 1 hour of chilling time)

These delicious cookies use a spiced molasses cookie dough, with one twist: they are coated in cinnamon and sugar just like a snickerdoodle!

GINGERDOODLE COOKIES

2⅓ cups (290 g) all-purpose flour, spooned and leveled

1 teaspoon baking soda

2 teaspoons ground ginger

1 teaspoon ground cinnamon

½ teaspoon ground cloves

¼ teaspoon salt

¾ cup (1½ sticks, or 170 g) unsalted butter, softened

1 cup (200 g) packed light brown sugar

1 large egg, at room temperature

¼ cup (75 g) unsulphured molasses

1 teaspoon pure vanilla extract

CINNAMON SUGAR COATING

¼ cup (50 g) granulated sugar

2 teaspoons ground cinnamon

PRO BAKING TIP
You can leave out the cinnamon in the coating for soft ginger molasses cookies.

---

1. **To make the gingerdoodle cookies:** In a large mixing bowl, whisk together the flour, baking soda, ground ginger, ground cinnamon, ground cloves, and salt until well combined. Set aside.

2. In the bowl of a stand mixer fitted with the paddle attachment or in a large mixing bowl using a handheld mixer, beat the butter and brown sugar together for 1 to 2 minutes, or until well combined.

3. Mix in the egg, molasses, and vanilla extract until fully combined, making sure to stop and scrape down the sides of the bowl as needed.

4. Mix in the dry ingredients until just combined.

5. Cover tightly and refrigerate for at least 1 hour.

6. Preheat the oven to 350°F (180°C). Line large baking sheets with parchment paper or silicone baking mats and set aside.

7. **To make the cinnamon sugar coating:** In a small mixing bowl, whisk together the ¼ cup (50 g) of granulated sugar and 2 teaspoons of ground cinnamon. Using a 1-tablespoon cookie scoop, scoop the cookie dough, roll it into a ball, and coat it in the cinnamon sugar mixture. Place each ball of cookie dough onto the prepared baking sheets, making sure to leave 1½ to 2 inches (4 to 5 cm) between each one.

8. Bake for 9 to 12 minutes, or until the tops of the cookies are set. Remove from the oven, and allow the cookies to cool on the baking sheets for 5 to 10 minutes, then carefully transfer the cookies to a wire rack to cool completely.

9. Store the cookies in an airtight container at room temperature for up to 1 week.

CRANBERRY ORANGE COOKIES

YIELD: 28 to 30 cookies

TOTAL TIME: 2 hours 43 minutes
(includes 2 hours of chilling time)

Orange can sometimes be an underrated flavor, but I personally love it. These delicious cookies are infused with orange zest and juice and then filled with sweetened dried cranberries.

2⅓ cups (290 g) all-purpose flour, spooned and leveled

½ teaspoon baking soda

¼ teaspoon salt

¾ cup (1½ sticks, or 170 g) unsalted butter, softened

1 cup (200 g) granulated sugar

¼ cup (50 g) packed light brown sugar

1 large egg, at room temperature

1 large egg yolk, at room temperature

1 teaspoon pure vanilla extract

Zest of 1 medium orange (2 teaspoons)

1 tablespoon (15 ml) fresh orange juice

1¼ cups (180 g) sweetened dried cranberries

1. In a large mixing bowl, whisk together the flour, baking soda, and salt until well combined. Set aside.

2. In the bowl of a stand mixer fitted with the paddle attachment or in a large mixing bowl using a handheld mixer, beat the butter, granulated sugar, and brown sugar together for 1 to 2 minutes, or until well combined.

3. Mix in the egg, egg yolk, and vanilla extract until well combined, then mix in the orange zest and orange juice until fully combined, making sure to stop and scrape down the sides of the bowl as needed.

4. Mix in the dry ingredients until just combined, then mix in the dried cranberries on low speed until fully incorporated.

5. Cover tightly and refrigerate for at least 2 hours.

6. Preheat the oven to 350°F (180°C). Line large baking sheets with parchment paper or silicone baking mats and set aside.

7. Using a 1½-tablespoon cookie scoop, scoop the cookie dough onto the prepared baking sheets, making sure to leave 1½ to 2 inches (4 to 5 cm) between each one.

8. Bake for 11 to 13 minutes, or until the tops of the cookie are set. Remove from the oven, and allow the cookies to cool on the baking sheets for 5 to 10 minutes, then carefully transfer the cookies to a wire rack to cool completely.

9. Store cookies in an airtight container at room temperature for up to 5 days.

PRO BAKING TIP

It's easier to zest your orange before you cut it and juice it. If you want to get more juice out of your orange, firmly roll it with your palm on the counter before cutting into it.

PEPPERMINT SNOWBALL COOKIES

YIELD: 34 to 36 cookies

TOTAL TIME: 49 minutes

NO CHILLING REQUIRED!

These snowball cookies are made with peppermint extract and a secret ingredient that's blended up and mixed with the powdered sugar for the coating. Can you guess what it is?

1 cup (2 sticks, or 230 g) unsalted butter, softened

1½ cups (180 g) powdered sugar, divided

1½ teaspoons peppermint extract

2¼ cups (280 g) all-purpose flour, spooned and leveled

¼ teaspoon salt

4 to 6 drops red liquid food coloring (optional)

2 regular-size candy canes (28 g)

PRO BAKING TIP

If you don't have a blender or small food processor to crush the candy canes, you can add them to a plastic bag and crush them with a rolling pin.

1. Preheat the oven to 350°F (180°C). Line two large baking sheets with parchment paper or silicone baking mats and set aside.

2. In the bowl of a stand mixer fitted with the paddle attachment or in a large mixing bowl using a handheld mixer, beat the butter and ½ cup (60 g) of the powdered sugar together for 1 to 2 minutes, or until well combined.

3. Add the peppermint extract and mix until fully combined, then mix in the flour and salt until just combined. Mix in a few drops of red food coloring (if using).

4. Using a 1-tablespoon cookie scoop, scoop the cookie dough onto the prepared baking sheets, making sure to leave 1½ to 2 inches (4 to 5 cm) between each one.

5. Bake for 12 to 14 minutes, or until the tops of the cookies are set. Remove from the oven, and allow the cookies to cool on the baking sheets for 5 to 10 minutes.

6. Add the candy canes to a blender or small food processor and grind into a fine powder.

7. Combine the candy cane powder and remaining 1 cup (120 g) powdered sugar in a large mixing bowl. Roll each cookie in the peppermint–powdered sugar mixture while it is still warm. Allow to cool completely, then roll all the cookies one more time.

8. Store the cookies in an airtight container at room temperature for up to 1 week.

BROWN SUGAR COOKIES

YIELD: 30 to 32 cookies

TOTAL TIME: 1 hour 42 minutes
(includes 1 hour of chilling time)

These sugar cookies are a fun spin on classic soft and chewy sugar cookies. Instead of using granulated sugar, they are made with light brown sugar, which lends them a softer texture and adds some molasses flavor. If you love brown sugar in your cookies, then be sure to give these a try!

2¾ cups (345 g) all-purpose flour, spooned and leveled

1 teaspoon baking soda

½ teaspoon ground cinnamon

½ teaspoon salt

1 cup (2 sticks, or 230 g) unsalted butter, softened

1⅓ cups (265 g) packed light brown sugar

1 large egg, at room temperature

1 large egg yolk, at room temperature

1½ teaspoons pure vanilla extract

3 tablespoons (40 g) granulated sugar, for coating (optional)

PRO BAKING TIP

The granulated sugar is completely optional, but I love the extra sweetness and crunch it adds to these cookies!

1. In a large mixing bowl, whisk together the flour, baking soda, ground cinnamon, and salt until well combined. Set aside.

2. In the bowl of a stand mixer fitted with the paddle attachment or in a large mixing bowl using a handheld mixer, beat the butter and brown sugar together for 1 to 2 minutes, or until well combined.

3. Mix in the egg, egg yolk, and vanilla extract until fully combined, making sure to stop and scrape down the sides of the bowl as needed.

4. Mix in the dry ingredients until just combined.

5. Cover tightly and refrigerate for at least 1 hour.

6. Preheat the oven to 350°F (180°C). Line large baking sheets with parchment paper or silicone baking mats.

7. Using a 1½-tablespoon cookie scoop, scoop the cookie dough, and coat it in the granulated sugar (if using). Place each ball of cookie dough onto the prepared baking sheets, making sure to leave 1½ to 2 inches (4 to 5 cm) between each one.

8. Bake for 10 to 12 minutes, or until the tops of the cookies are set and the edges are lightly browned. Remove from the oven, and allow the cookies to cool on the baking sheets for 5 to 10 minutes, then carefully transfer the cookies to a wire rack to cool completely.

9. Store the cookies in an airtight container at room temperature for up to 1 week.

INDEX

ACKNOWLEDGMENTS

While I spent countless hours working on this cookbook, I certainly would not have been able to do this all on my own.

I want to thank my husband, Josh, for helping me test, retest, and photograph all the cookie recipes in this cookbook. Thank you for helping me wash all the dishes, always being my biggest supporter, and believing in my crazy dream of becoming a full-time food blogger.

I would also like to thank everyone at The Quarto Group who helped bring this book to life, specifically Erin Canning, Todd Conly, and Rage Kindelsperger. I appreciate your patience working with me on my first cookbook and always being so helpful!

Last, but certainly not least, I want to thank all my readers who have made and trusted my recipes over the last seven years. Without you, this cookbook wouldn't have been possible, and I wouldn't be able to do what I love every single day. I'm so truly grateful for each and every one of you!

ABOUT THE AUTHOR

Danielle Rye is the recipe creator and blogger behind the website Live Well Bake Often. Started in 2014 as a way to share her love for baking, Live Well Bake Often has become a community for bakers of all skill levels to find easy and delicious homemade recipes for any event or holiday.

Growing a business that helps everyone bake tasty treats while gaining confidence in the kitchen has been one of Danielle's dreams. On her website, she continues to share her extensive baking knowledge with her readers, making Live Well Bake Often a comprehensive resource for all things baking.

When she is not baking, Danielle enjoys traveling and hiking with her husband and dogs. You can find all of her delicious recipes on her website, livewellbakeoften.com, or her Instagram, @livewellbakeoften.